Environmental Planning:
An Economic Analysis

James C. Hite
Eugene A. Laurent

Published in cooperation with
The Conservation Foundation and
the Coastal Plains Regional Commission

The Praeger Special Studies program—utilizing the most modern and efficient book production techniques and a selective worldwide distribution network—makes available to the academic, government, and business communities significant, timely research in U.S. and international economic, social, and political development.

Environmental Planning:
An Economic Analysis
Applications for
the Coastal Zone

PRAEGER SPECIAL STUDIES IN U.S. ECONOMIC AND SOCIAL DEVELOPMENT

Praeger Publishers   New York   Washington   London

PRAEGER PUBLISHERS
111 Fourth Avenue, New York, N.Y. 10003, U.S.A.
5, Cromwell Place, London S.W.7, England

Published in the United States of America in 1972
by Praeger Publishers, Inc.

Library of Congress Catalog Card Number: 72-75698

Printed in the United States of America

This report was prepared in accordance
with contract No. 10042023 of the Coastal
Plains Regional Commission and
The Conservation Foundation. Funds to
support the empirical research reported
herein were made available under a grant
from the Office of Water Resources
Research, U.S. Department of the Interior

Our research into the economic problems of coastal zone manage-
ment began almost three years ago at Clemson University with a series
of specialized studies of the commercial fisheries of the South Atlantic
states. Out of those fisheries studies, there grew a major interest
in applying economic analysis to the very difficult problems of resource allocation and conservation in the coastal zone. In 1969, the
senior author received a grant from the Office of Water Resources
Research, U.S. Department of the Interior, to study the economic
implications of various schemes for zoning coastal areas. It was
this grant that made possible the expensive collection of empirical
data related to the Charleston, South Carolina, economy, which is
reported in this book. As we worked with problems in the coastal
zone, however, we became increasingly aware of the need to adapt
the existing body of economic theory to help answer the problems
which face planners and public administrators charged with managing
coastal resources. During the academic year 1969-70, the senior
author was able to study these broader problems as a member of the
Regional Science Group at Harvard University. This book is the
result of our experience and study to date.

The study is not written for the professional economist, although
it is hoped the economist will find it interesting. Rather it is written
as a handbook for planners and public administrators. Consequently,
an effort has been made to avoid unnecessary technical and theoretical
discussions. Yet we have felt the need to develop the body of economic
logic that applies to resource problems in the coastal zone and to
diagnose these problems as legitimate matters of economic concern.
Our purpose here is to refute the notion widely held by noneconomists
that economic science is concerned only with pecuniary problems and
that it can make no contribution to discussion of management decisions
which must consider nonpecuniary values.

Eugene Laurent, the junior author and a former Ph.D. candidate
in natural resource economics at Clemson University, prepared a
doctoral thesis in connection with the economic evaluation of zoning
alternatives in coastal areas. He has had principal responsibilities
for the collection and processing of the empirical data and for construction of the Charleston area input-output matrix. In every case,
however, where a conflict of views arose, the senior author has

exerted privileges of a graduate adviser and has overruled his student. The senior author assumes full responsibility for the study.

There are many more persons to whom acknowledgments are due than we can possibly enumerate. We will mention only those who were associated with the project over some period of time. James M. Stepp, W. J. Lanham, and John S. Lytle at Clemson University, Walter Isard and John Kissin at Harvard University, Joseph L. Gabbard of the Coastal Plains Regional Commission, and Ann Satterthwaite of The Conservation Foundation have offered encouragement and support throughout the duration of this project. Marvin G. Carmichael, Lee H. Covey, Donald Lovette, and William J. Steele assisted with the field work in the collection of the data. Finally, special acknowledgment is due Cary Singleton of the Department of Agricultural Economics and Rural Sociology at Clemson who typed several versions of this study with patience and skill.

PART IV: SYNTHESIS AND APPLICATION

LIST OF TABLES

xii

LIST OF FIGURES

DIAGNOSIS
OF THE
PROBLEM

1

INTRODUCTION
TO RESOURCE PROBLEMS
IN
THE COASTAL ZONE

POLICY PROBLEMS IN THE COASTAL ZONE

Protection of the environment—e. g., the conservation of natural resources—has become a pressing policy issue in the United States in the second half of the twentieth century. The coastal zone has been a critical site for the joining of this issue, primarily because of the many conflicting demands for a relatively scarce supply of shoreline and related coastal amenities. At one extreme in the controversy are the "preservationists," who contend that all coastal resources should be preserved in some natural state and used only for limited access recreational purposes (if used at all). At the other extreme are the "exploiters," who demand that all resources be used for purposes of economic development, as measured by increases in immediate or short-run per capita dollar income and the number of jobs. Each extreme seems to insist adamantly that the only policy which will serve well the long-run interests of the American people is one that exclusively accepts its position. Policy-makers and planners at all government levels are caught in the middle between these two extreme positions, and they are very vulnerable to pressures from either extreme because they have no objective basis for evaluating the trade-offs between the two extremes and, thus, defining an optimum system of uses for the resources of the coastal zone.

Physically, the coastal zone may be defined as a rather narrow transitional ribbon occurring where a continental land mass meets a tidal sea. To the biologist, this ribbon is one of the most productive zones on the globe. With the possible exception fo the crops of rice and sugar cane, no commerical agriculture can come close to matching the productivity per acre of this area in the production of potential food for animals.[1] To the geographer, the coastal zone is a buffer

for the most densely inhabited land areas of the earth from the violence
of the sea.[2] To the sportsman, the coastal zone is a splendid habitat
for many species of water birds, sport fishes, and other game. To
the commercial fishermen, it is a nursery ground for many of the
most valuable species, such as shrimp and oysters. To the developer,
the coastal zone is a potential space where new residences can be built
next to the sparkling blue waters of the sea. To the artist, it is an
ever changing mirage of color—vast green savannas of marsh grass
and roaring, robust waves of breaking surf. The coastal zone is,
thus, a major natural resource, or bundle of resources, of immense
value for commercial, recreational, and aesthetic reasons.

The many views of the coastal zone and its resources pose three
very significant policy problems: (1) To what use, or combination of
uses, is the coastal zone to be devoted? (2) What individuals, or firms,
will be allowed to engage in these uses? (3) Who will administer the
allocation of coastal resources among the various uses? Such problems,
of course, are not unique to the resources of the coastal zone. They
are general problems which arise whenever a resource, or group of
resources, is scarce relative to all the many uses to which it may be
put. And they are problems whose solution falls within the general
realm of economic problems usually described in elementary economics
textbooks as: what shall be produced, how much shall be produced,
and who shall produce it. Yet the problems of the coastal zone, like
the general problem of environmental quality, are not well-suited to
solution by the standard economic mechanisms of an open market and
the price system. This is true not only because many of the products
of the coastal zone are not subject to market exchange but also because
the institutional imperfections of the market are especially serious
in the allocation of what we shall later define as environmental goods.
Thus, the management of the coastal zone has generally fallen into
the public sector of the economy.

When resource management falls into this sector, it becomes
subject to a great variety of political pressures which may, or may
not, tend to push policy toward extremes suggested by criteria of
economic efficiency. The self-interest which is more or less explicit
as a motivating force in the market becomes hidden behind the holy
robes of crusaders who agitate with great self-righteous zeal. As
noted by Professors James Stepp and Hugh Macaulay, "The zeal of
the crusader can serve a necessary and useful purpose in awakening
citizens and public officials to the necessity of dealing with problems
that have gradually, almost imperceptibly, reached serious proportions
[but] in many situations the public interest is better served by an
analytical approach than by a crusading one."[3] The policy problems
of the coastal zone are, thus, likely to be settled in an atmosphere

of charged emotions and political log-rolling. At least, they can be
expected to represent something of a compromise between economic
efficiency and political necessity. In this study, however, we will
confine ourselves to an "analytical approach" using the conventional
tools of economic analysis.

USE CONFLICTS IN THE COASTAL ZONE

The problems of public management of the resources of the
coastal zone arise because those resources have become scarce relative to the demand for their use. Heavy industry seeks a water-front
location so as to have access to ocean-going commerce and a cheap
source of industrial water; bathers and sports fishermen head to the
coastal areas to find opportunities for relaxation and recreation; coastal
municipalities seek low-cost means of disposing of solid waste in the
adjacent marshland; and nature-lovers covet the vast open spaces of
coastal wilderness. If there were more than enough coastal resources
to satisfy these and other demands, there would be little need for any
public management program. And, throughout much of our history,
there were no serious use conflicts in the coastal zone. The traditional
uses were few and not intense. Commercial fishermen, recreationists,
and shippers seldom got in each other's way; there was enough coast
for all who desired to use its resources.

But the growth of population and industry has increased both
the number and the intensity of potential users of the coastal zone.
The density of oil drilling platforms off the Gulf Coast, for example,
has become so great that the U.S. Coast Guard and the Army Corps
of Engineers have had to intervene to establish fairways for shipping.
Housing development has drastically changed the coastal zone in the
Boca Ciega Bay area off the west coast of Florida. Filling of marsh-
lands by spoil from the dredging of navigation channels and for purposes
of creating high land has cut heavily onto the estuarine habitat needed
for both sport and commercial fishing.[4] These use conflicts are both
temporal and spatial—that is, they arise from competing desires of
some for space in the coastal zone to be used now and of others to
reserve space for future needs, which currently cannot be fully
anticipated.

In general, combinations of uses of any resource can be classified into three categories: (1) complementary, (2) supplementary, and
(3) competitive.[5] Complementary use activities are those in which
an increase in the level of one activity will increase the productive
potential of the other activities. An example might be the channel

maintenance for commercial shipping which also improves opportunities for recreation boating—an example readily noted in the case of the Atlantic Intercoastal Waterway. Use activities are supplementary when change in the level of one activity has no effect on the level of activity of other uses. Recreational boating and commercial fishing are normally supplementary within some range of activity. Competitive activities are those which hinder each other, for example, commercial fishing and waste disposal.

One of the first problems, therefore, is to determine just which activities are complementary, which are supplementary, and which are competitive. But that is not an easy problem to solve. In the extreme, almost all activities are competitive. That is, if commercial shipping becomes very great, it will interfere with recreational boating, and vice versa. By the same token, even waste disposal and commercial fishing may be complementary if the levels of both activities are relatively low, since the waste often enriches the water and increases its productivity for aquatic life. Conflicts never arise until the levels of two or more activities have reached the point that they become competitive for some scarce resource. As the demand for use of coastal resource increases, more and more uses are likely to become competitive. These conflicts, in and of themselves, are not undesirable, because, from an economic standpoint, no resource is being fully utilized until conflicts arise over its use.[6] But, when these conflicts arise over resources not subject to a free competitive market, careful public management is necessary to prevent a misallocation of the resources.

PUBLIC AGENCIES IN THE COASTAL ZONE

There is a bewildering array of public agencies which have either legal and/or traditional responsibilities for management of certain resources of the coastal zone. Some of the agencies are federal, some state, some local. A task force studying tidelands policy in South Carolina discovered that twenty state and federal agencies were charged with some type of management responsibility for the resources of the coastal zone of that state.[7] The federal government has jurisdiction over submerged land and navigable waters under the navigation and commerce clauses of the Constitution. There is also a federal interest in the coastal zone as it pertains to national defense, flood control, and electrical power production. The several states exercise police powers over the coastal zone; they build roads, bridges, and causeways, regulate hunting and fishing, establish pollution standards, maintain public parks and other recreational facilities, and grant title to land. Local governments may have zoning ordinances which regulate the coastal areas. In many cases, the jurisdictional boundaries between the responsibilities of these agencies are not clear. There are wide areas of responsibility which are not assigned to any agency and other areas where assigned responsibilities overlap.

The institutional nature of resource problems in the coastal zone, especially as it pertains to public agencies, can perhaps best be appreciated by the example of South Carolina. As in most states, the government of South Carolina has taken the general position that title to all lands below the mean high-tide mark is vested in the state and that these lands (including submerged lands and navigable waters) are held in trust for the public. An exception to this position is recognized, however, in the case of some royal grants which specifically included tidal lands. In the latter cases, private title is recognized if a claimant can bring into court a chain of title back to the original grant from the sovereign. Since the tidal lands have historically not been considered of great value, the state has failed to inventory the extent of its claim and there is considerable confusion as to just how much land is still held by the state. All title to these lands, however, is subject to the paramount rights of the federal government under the U.S. Constitution.[8] This confusion as to title has been an important hindrance in public efforts to develop recreational facilities and control beach erosion since such investments can be made only if the facilities or beach is open to public access.

Aside from the question of legal title, management of the coastal resources of South Carolina is also being frustrated by agency conflicts. Four state agencies, for example, exercise legislative authority to grant or lease state lands for specific purposes. The State Development Board has authority to provide land for the deposit of spoil from the dredging of the Intercoastal Waterway; the State Ports Authority has authority for providing spoil areas for navigation channel maintenance for the three state ports; the Wildlife Resource Commission can lease lands for oyster production; and the State Budget and Control Board can lease lands for mining and other purposes. In the latter case, there is no clear limit on the uses for which the Budget and Control Board may make state property available. Most of the dredging for navigation purposes is accomplished by the U.S. Army Corps of Engineers. As a consequence of this division of authority, the Development Board, the Ports Authority, the Budget and Control Board, and the Corps of Engineers often find themselves in conflict with the Wildlife Commission.[9] Other state agencies, such as the Department of Parks, Recreation, and Tourism and the State Highway Department have authority (and responsibility) for developing structures

in the coastal zone which change the environment by interrupting tidal
flow and emitting various sorts of pollutants.

The diffusion of responsibility and authority is not unique to
South Carolina or even to the states in general. The U.S. Coast
Guard, the Army Corps of Engineers, the Soil Conservation Service,
the Forest Service, the Environmental Protection Agency (EPA), the
National Park Service, and many other federal agencies also have a
special interest in the management of the coastal zone. State agencies
tend to deal directly with their counterparts at the federal level, and
prior to the enactment of the National Environmental Policy Act of
1969 and subsequent executive orders of the President, all these
agencies tended to act independently of each other (except in cases
where coordination was clearly unavoidable). The National Environment Protection Act, which established the Council on Environmental
Quality in the Executive Office of the President, introduces an element
of coordination and order into federal activities concerning the environment.[10] The Executive Order of President Richard Nixon setting up
the EPA provides an administrative framework for making better
coordination a reality.[11]

A CONCEPTUAL APPROACH TO COASTAL
ZONE MANAGEMENT

A conceptual approach to the management of coastal resources
is necessary if "maximum returns" to society are to be realized from
these resources. The concept of "multiple use" is frequently set
forth as a type of management system. Multiple use means that an
effort is made to accommodate two or more uses within the same
area. It is an attempt to reach a balance between the desire to develop
resources and the need to preserve resources. However, we must
recognize that all uses considered are not the same in their effects
on coastal areas. Some uses of the tidelands cause changes in the
coastal environment which are permanent and irreversible. Other
uses are only temporary in their effect, and when they are stopped
the area will revert quickly to its prior natural state. A wildlife
area, for example, can always be converted into an industrial area
or a spoil area. But it is much more difficult to convert an established
industrial or spoil area into other uses. Thus, the use of coastal
areas for activities which involve long-range commitments to a particular use should be given careful study as this can effectively exclude
many other uses. This is not to say that long-range irreversible
activities should be disallowed. They may be very necessary, but
we should carefully consider such uses and understand their future
effects on the benefits from the area.

The adoption of a multiple use plan for public management for our coastal areas is not enough. A truly comprehensive management program should incorporate the following considerations:

1. an inventory of resources to know where we are and to provide the basis for understanding the effects one type of activity has on another;

2. priorities among goals and, if there is more than one goal, general priorities for tradeoffs between them;

3. priorities for uses both in terms of their relevant economic importance and their importance over a period of time;

4. the tools and methods of organizing data for decision purposes, so the data fit the methods of analysis used to deal with problems;

5. openness and flexibility with respect to identification of all problems, exploitation of alternative courses of action, and incorporation of the new research needed to overcome our fragmented knowledge.

A comprehensive management system should also meet several general objectives including: (1) ensuring to the state the maximum present and future returns from coastal resources in light of some stated goal or goals; (2) balancing the rights of the present generation against the rights of future generations; and (3) allocating powers and duties as clearly as possible between the private and public sectors.

A comprehensive (multiple-use) management plan for the coastal zone must have goals established, an overriding philosophy or system in which individual decisions can be placed, and a clear idea of an analytical tool for organizing data to aid in decision-making.

In the following chapters, we shall explore some possibilities for the use of economic reasoning in the formulation of techniques useful in implementing a systems approach to environmental planning in the coastal zone.

NOTES

1. John and Mildred Teal, Life and Death of a Salt Marsh (Boston: Atlantic Monthly Press, 1969), p. 198.

2. L. Eugene Cronin, "The Role of Man in Estuarine Processes,"
in George H. Lauff, ed. Estuaries (Washington, D.C.: American
Association for the Advancement of Science, 1967), p. 667.

3. J. M. Stepp and H. H. Macaulay, The Pollution Problem
(Washington, D.C.: American Enterprise Institute, 1968), pp. 20-21.

4. Our Nation and the Sea: A Plan for National Action, Report
of the Commission on Marine Science, Engineering Resources (Washington, D.C.: U.S. Government Printing Office, January, 1969), pp.
49-50.

5. This section follows very closely Niels Rorholm, Economic
Impact of Narragansett Bay (Kingston: University of Rhode Island
Experiment Station, December, 1963), pp. 16-17.

6. Ibid., p. 7.

7. South Carolina Tidelands Report (Columbia: South Carolina
Water Resources Commission, 1969), p. 11.

8. Ibid., pp. 21-22.

9. Ibid., p. 6.

10. See Appendix A, Environmental Quality, The First Annual
Report of the Council on Environmental Quality (Washington, D.C.,
U.S. Government Printing Office, August, 1970), pp. 243-49.

11. See Appendix H, Ibid., pp. 294-305.

In Chapter 1 we reviewed in summary and nontechnical fashion the policy problems which have arisen in the coastal zone. In this chapter we will begin a more systematic examination of those problems. Specifically, we will attempt to analyze the noncommercial products of the coastal zone as a peculiar kind of economic good, looking at ways in which these products are similar to more orthodox economic products and the ways in which they are different.

ECONOMICS AND THE ENVIRONMENT

Economics is the science of values and choices. As a field of scholarly pursuit, it is concerned with the way in which individuals and society allocate the scarce resources which are available in order to obtain the maximum satisfaction of human wants. For reasons of convenience, most economic discussion centers around pecuniary values and pecuniary choices. But that is only because money is a useful index for expressing values. There are many other values which are not easily translated into the money index but, nevertheless, are amenable to economic analysis. Among these are the values associated with environmental goods.

What do we mean by environmental goods? The environment is, in a very real sense, a complete natural and social system. All its parts are ecologically interrelated to one another, and, for many purposes, it is useful to discuss the environment in its totality. But our thinking can be expedited if we also conceive of the environment as a bundle of useful, or potentially useful, natural resources, each of which is capable of producing two types of economic goods. The first of these types we may style <u>pecuniary goods</u>, meaning that they are

11

marketable in some way and thus flow through the commercial sectors of the economy. The second type might be called environmental goods. Included in this latter category would be such things as clean air, clean water, panoramic vistas, etc. Environmental goods possess value which is just as real as that of pecuniary goods, but that value is not normally or completely measured in the marketplace and, thus, not normally completely translated into a monetary index.

Economists have considerable experience in dealing with pecuniary goods. A body of theory has developed which provides criteria for evaluating the efficiency of the allocation of resources when the products of those resources can be priced in a free and competitive market. If the market is perfectly competitive, the values of society can be imputed from the market exchange price. But, since environmental goods are not completely marketable, their value is more difficult to impute in any objective way. The lack of reliable market mechanisms for defining the value of environmental goods, however, does not imply that their value is zero, nor does it imply that it is infinite. An unfinished task of economics is to determine the appropriate values of particular environmental goods so as to judge better how natural resources should be allocated among all the potential users who desire their services.

THE NATURE OF ENVIRONMENTAL GOODS

Natural resources may be thought of as a form of capital. In pure theory, capital has been defined as "the aggregate of things which are capable of yielding a stream of services extending into the future . . ."[1] Like other forms of capital, it is not the physical nature of the natural resources that is important, but the stream of services which society can draw from the resources over time.[2] The natural resource endowment of any nation or region has no intrinsic value, in and of itself. The value arises only out of the contributions those resources can make to human welfare. This concept of resources as capital has not been fully understood either by many public administrators or by conservation groups, many of whom seemed to be more concerned about the preservation of natural resources than their wise use. There is some truth to J. K. Galbraith's wry definition of a conservationist as "a man who concerns himself with the beauties of nature in roughly inverse proportion to the number of people who can enjoy them."[3]

Two different types of use can be had of a given natural resource: (1) It can be converted from its natural form into some other form of

capital—e.g., marsh can be filled with spoil from the dredging of a
navigation channel, thus increasing the flow of transportation services
but decreasing the flow of marsh services, or (2) it can be utilized in
its natural state. In the natural state, for example, marsh serves as
a nursery ground for several important species of commercial fish
and shellfish, which are pecuniary goods, and it also provides aesthetic
pleasure and buffers the land from storms, two services which are
environmental goods. The conversion of natural resources into some
other form of capital is often irreversible. It is not easy, for example,
to restore a marsh once it has been filled by spoil. Yet most of man's
material progress has involved "converting natural resources into
more desirable forms of wealth,"[4] and surely the general quality of
human life would be much lower if man had never felled a tree or dug
a ditch.

Some natural resources are easily subject to exclusive appropriation under the rules of private property, as, for example, are
land, forest products, and access to a stream. Others, including
such resources as the air, the oceans, and the bottoms of streams,
fall into a category of common property. These latter resources
may be used by all who care to use them, and no single user can
prevent anyone else from sharing in their exploitation. Furthermore,
no one individual user of a common-property resource can be assured
that, if he leaves some of the resource for later use, it will be available to him when he returns. A common-property resource may
produce either pecuniary goods or environmental goods or both.
Regardless, there is a tendency for the cost of using a common-
property resource by any one individual to be below the value which
society as a whole places on the goods that resource is producing.

Certain natural resources have remained common-property
resources either because it has not been technically possible to appropriate and defend the resources for private use, or because, if it were
technically possible, the expected returns from such private use would
not justify the cost associated with doing so. In many cases, of course,
both reasons have been present. For example, it technically is not
very easy to appropriate and defend some portion of the atmosphere.
But even if technology provided means by which such a feat could be
accomplished, the vast abundance of air relative to the needs of any
one individual or firm has not made exclusive appropriation a very
urgent need.[5]

As long as any common-property resource is really abundant
relative to the demand for its use, one may wonder why there should
be economic problems of allocation. As we noted in Chapter 1, the

natural resources of the coastal zone were historically so abundant
that until recently no general problem of conflict was observable.
But, as we also noted, use conflicts are now amply evident in the
coastal zone. Perhaps no more dramatic example exists than that of
the Potomac estuary. The pollution of the Potomac, largely by domestic waste from the Washington metropolitan area, has received national
attention in the press and is rightly viewed as a grave national problem.
The waste assimilative capacity of the Potomac is limited, even if
rather lax water quality standards are established. Yet the population
of the Washington area continues to grow and the domestic waste of
that population must somehow be disposed of. The Potomac estuary
is an obvious sink for such disposal and is in demand for the removal
of these wastes. By the same token, the Potomac estuary is also in
demand for recreation purposes—boating, swimming, fishing, etc.—
and these recreational uses are not compatible with the use of the
estuary as a sink for sewage. Present levels of sewage treatment
for the Washington area are not high enough to maintain the river in
a condition suitable for recreational uses, and, with the expected
population growth of the area, treatment levels must be increased
drastically over the next decade to prevent water quality in the Potomac
estuary from deteriorating even further. To restore the Potomac to
a level of quality consistent with that required for recreation will be
enormously expensive, in terms of engineering costs associated with
more and more sophisticated treatment facilities and/or a halt in (and
even reversal of) the population growth in the Potomac basin.

The people who are responsible for the domestic waste that
pollutes the Potomac are, in many cases, also the same people who
desire use of the estuary for recreation. These polluters may find
the condition of the water there just as deplorable as the most con-
firmed naturalist. The polluters are apt to decry with great sincerity
the lack of clean water for fishing, boating, and swimming. Why, then,
do they persist in contributing to the general pollution problem? The
answer is that any restraint in pollution of the Potomac estuary (or
any other common-property resource) by one individual will probably
have only a negligible effect on the total quality of the estuary. That
is, the incremental damage to the Potomac of any one person or household is so small relative to the gain in stream quality resulting from
restraint that the individual is not motivated to take personal action.

In the absence of a general restraint on particular uses of a
common-property resource, the action of an individual firm or person
will only result in a forfeiture of whatever advantages he is receiving
from exploitation of the resource without any compensating improvement
in the quantity of the resource available for alternative long- or

short-run uses. If the individual were able to exercise exclusive control over the resource, he would have greater incentive to conserve
its supply, but, as long as the natural resource is a common-property
resource, anything he leaves will be taken by other users.6

Of course, not all problems associated with the misallocation
of environmental goods arise because some of them are common-
property resources. Problems also arise because some of the effects
of particular decisions about the use of some natural resources may
fall on persons other than those who make the decisions. A landowner
may choose to build a tall building on his lot and shade his neighbor's
backyard swimming pool, for example. In such a case, part of the
"costs" of erecting the tall building are not born by the builder, but
by his neighbor who is no longer able to sun by his pool and who then
loses an environmental good. If the builder is forced to pay damages
for the sunlight which the pool owner loses, he may decide the expected
benefits from the extra height of the tall building will not equal or exceed the cost (including damages done to his neighbor) of adding the
extra height. But, if the builder is not liable for such damages, he
is under no incentive to consider the harmful effects which the building
may have on others.7 Economists call such effects externalities, since
they are external to the decision-making process.

Externalities which arise out of the exercise of private property
rights can be handled by litigation in courts of equity. The swimming
pool owner may sue the builder of the next-door high-rise and attempt
to collect damages. Likewise, the riparian owner of land may sue an
upstream polluter if the latter's use of the stream is unreasonable
and recover damages or obtain a cease-and-desist order relative to
the pollution activities. When private property rights are matters of
settled legal principle, a judicial system and appropriate laws of
liability can function to solve many of the problems posed by the externalities on the use of environmental goods.8 Yet property rights
are not settled principles when an environmental good is the product
of a common-property resource. No one has a property right to the
air or to the ocean, or to wild animals, or to a particular view.
Consequently, no one can sue for damages resulting to a piece of property to which he has no more claim than the user who offends him.

THE COASE PROBLEM AND
ENVIRONMENTAL GOODS

Traditional economic analysis of externalities, following the
work of A. C. Pigou, has usually viewed harmful externalities as a

social cost not accounted for by the private cost of the individual or firm inflicting the externality.9 Implicit in this analysis is the judgment that the creator of the externalities is an offender against society and that damages are one-directional in their effect. Professor Ronald N. Coase has argued that such analysis is not logically sound.10 As Coase sees the problem, there is a reciprocal relationship to social cost. For example, an oysterman may use a mechanical harvester to dredge up oysters from the mud banks and flats and, in doing so, disturb the surface so as to reduce the potential of the marsh as a nursery ground for shrimp. Thus, the oysterman reduces the shrimp harvest potential for shrimpers and inflicts damages upon the shrimper. Yet preservation of the marsh bottom for shrimp production excludes the use of the mechanical harvester by the oysterman and thus inflicts damages upon him. Damages are, in fact, two-directional and there is no logical basis for determining which use has priority.

There are, of course, a large number of schemes for arbitrarily establishing a priority for uses of a common-property natural resource. One very obvious possibility is prior appropriation or the doctrine of priority of occupation. Such a scheme would tend to protect traditional users at the expense of new uses or technological innovations associated with other established uses. That is, the oysterman and shrimper may continue to use the marsh as long as the oysterman refraines from introducing a mechanical harvester and continues to harvest oysters by primitive hand methods. Such a doctrine, therefore, would greatly retard technological development which might lead to increases in the total productivity of the marshland. The priority of occupation doctrine would mean, therefore, as Professor Mason Gaffney has noted, that resources would be forever committed to traditional uses "at whatever costs to all concerned."11 From an economic standpoint, such a scheme is highly undesirable.

Coase proceeds from his analysis of the reciprocal nature of social costs to show that, under certain market assumptions, it is not necessary to identify a one-directional line of damage. The real question, according to Coase, is not who is responsible for the damage but who should be allowed to damage whom. And the economic problem is "to avoid the most serious harm."12 Let us continue our example of the oysterman and the shrimper to illustrate the Coase analysis. Assume the savings per annum, which the oysterman can realize by use of a mechanical harvester (rather than harvest by hand) is $1,000. Now also assume that the reduction in the value of the shrimp harvest resulting from the use of the mechanical oyster harvester is $2,000 per annum. Further assume for the present that there is only one oysterman and one shrimper and that the costs of market transportation

between the two is zero. Now what is the logical solution to the problem?
The shrimper has more to gain from the oysterman not using the mechanical harvester than the oysterman stands to gain from its use.
So the shrimper will approach the oysterman and bargain with him in
an attempt to "bribe" him into not using the mechanical harvester.
Assuming each party knows the cost figures mentioned above, the
oysterman will be willing to not use the mechanical oyster harvester
if the shrimper offers him $1,000 or more. And, as long as the
shrimper does not pay the oysterman more than $2,000 to get him to
stop using the oyster harvester, he stands to gain from striking a
bargain. Since the "most serious harm" is inflicted on the shrimper,
the bargain will serve to avoid that harm. At the same time, the
shrimper will be forced to consider the harmful effect which his activity has on the technological innovation in the oyster industry.

The rather restricting assumptions associated with the example
of the Coase analysis above are not very relevant to the real world,
however. Seldom are there only two parties associated with some
conflict over the use of a common-property environmental good.
Assume, for example, that we have only one oysterman who can save
$1,000 per annum by using a mechanical harvester, but ten shrimpers
who in the aggregate will lose $2,000 per annum if the harvester is
used. For purposes of simplification, assume each of these shrimpers
shares equally in the potential loss—that is, they each stand to lose
$200 per annum. What difference does this change in assumptions
make to the Coase solution? Clearly no one shrimper can now afford
to offer a large enough bribe to the oysterman to provide him adequate
incentive to not use his mechanical harvester. The shrimpers can
afford an acceptable bribe only if at least five of them pool their resources and approach the oysterman. Even if at least five of the
shrimpers could organize to bribe the oysterman, there would be
extra costs associated with this organization and with collection of
the funds from the individual shrimpers. Therefore, the assumption
that the costs of the market transaction—i.e., the bribe, the bargain—
is zero must also be dropped. More important, however, is the
possibility of some shrimpers becoming "free-riders."[13]

As long as at least five shrimpers get together to strike a bargain
with the oysterman, there is no incentive for other shrimpers to contribute to the pool. These shrimpers can have a free ride. Moreover,
since every individual shrimper may see himself as a possible free-
rider, or, alternatively, as the stooge who pays while others obtain
a free ride, there may be little incentive for the shrimpers to even
undertake to strike a bargain with the oysterman. Each shrimper
may adopt what Professor James Buchanan calls the "let George do

it" attitude, with the result that no transaction takes place at all. [14]
Such an attitude is especially likely if the number of shrimpers ad-
versely affected by the mechanical harvester is so large that few of
them personally interact with each other. [15]

We could complicate the Coase analysis even further by dropping
the assumption of one oysterman. By the same token, we could also
drop the assumption that all parties to the conflict perceive the costs
associated with alternative courses of action open to them. Such complications would only further serve to show why the free market fails
to allocate common-property resources in accordance with generally
accepted notions of economic efficiency. Yet Coase does point the
way by which a condition of economic efficiency might be approximated
by the introduction of certain nonmarket institutions which can facilitate
the kinds of payments that might be forthcoming if all the complications
which interfere with Coase's solutions were not present.

ENVIRONMENTAL GOODS AS PUBLIC GOODS

The preceding analysis leads to the conclusion that those environmental goods which flow from common-property natural resources
must be supplied through institutions other than the market. There
are, of course, many products or services other than those we have
styled environmental goods which also are supplied through nonmarket
institutions—police protection, national defense, and freeways are a
few examples. Such products and services have been classified by
economists as public goods, and a rather significant body of theory
has been developed to explain their allocation.

What are public goods? Professor Paul Samuelson defines pure
public goods as those "which all enjoy in common in the sense that
each individual's consumption of such a good leads to no subtraction
from any other individual's consumption of that good. "[16] Samuelson's
definition is rather restrictive in the sense that it allows for no conflicts over use of a resource. For example, an individual's use of a
highway may add to the traffic congestion and subtract from the consumption of highway services by another individual. Buchanan, however, has defined public goods in a broader fashion as "those goods
that are demanded and supplied through political institutions rather
than through market institutions. "[17] It is in this latter sense that we
can consider many environmental goods as public goods.

It certainly seems in order, however, to note that not all environmental goods must necessarily be public goods even under the Buchanan
definition. Those services flowing from natural resources which are

subject to the laws of private property may be obtained through market institutions. Wealthy sportsmen have long maintained their own private hunting preserves and, in doing so, have purchased the environmental good of recreational hunting. One might conceivably buy up large tracts of land to preserve and enjoy some scenic attraction that he especially enjoys or to obtain a rustic, natural surrounding. By the same token, of course, one might also hire his own police force or build his own roads. The absolute cost of obtaining environmental goods in this way, however, is so high that most citizens cannot expect to obtain them privately. They look to a collective purchase through their government and bring political pressure for public parks, game management areas, etc. Thus, some environmental goods are public goods because they are conventionally demanded through such institutions.

If one has enough wealth and is so minded, it is conceptually possible to imagine how one might buy clean air and clean water by bribing polluters until they ceased their pollution activities. We noted this possibility in examining the Coase analysis, but we also noted that there would be many free-riders who would benefit from such a bribe. Unlike the hunting preserve or the secluded estate, clean air and clean water cannot be exclusively appropriated for private use and enjoyment. Thus, even very wealthy people are inclined to seek to spread the cost of obtaining these environmental goods by looking to collective political action rather than to a private bribe.

There is a cost associated with supplying any public good which is just as real as the cost associated with supplying goods in the marketplace. Clean air and water can be supplied only at the cost of not using the atmosphere and water as a repository for waste. Public parks and beaches can be supplied only if such land is purchased and reserved by the government, with the resulting loss of the opportunity to use those lands for other purposes. One of the chief problems associated with public goods is that those who pay the cost of their being supplied may not benefit proportionately (or even significantly) from their being supplied. For example, nonusers of beach areas may have to pay, through their taxes, for the maintenance of beach areas which only a few bathers will enjoy. Those who do not care for beach recreation will have to provide tax funds to provide this environmental good for those who do enjoy the sun and the surf. It can be argued that the hunters and surf-bathers may pay taxes which pay for public goods they do not use and that, in the end, it all averages out. But there is no necessary reason why it should all average out, and, since users of environmental goods may not have to pay the full cost of supplying that good, they are apt to demand more of it than they would if they were forced to calculate whether the cost of supplying the additional units of the good were less than the benefits they believed they would derive from having it available. The point is that environmental goods become, in themselves, common property so that the individual cost of using more of them is often less than the social cost associated with providing more of those goods. There is no built-in check on consumption.

In the case of some public goods, a built-in partial check on consumption has been achieved through the mechanism of user charges. Toll bridges and highways are examples of user charges on public goods. The "Golden Eagle" sticker for automobiles of persons using camping facilities in the national parks and forests is an example of the application of user charges to environmental goods; hunting and fishing licenses are additional examples. In the case of the highway tolls, the charges are more or less proportionate to the amount of use; the more one uses the highway, the more toll one pays. Stickers and licenses, however, are flat, one-time user charges; there are no incremental charges associated with additional camping, hunting, or fishing. Thus, these stickers and licenses are only partially effective as checks on overconsumption. They ration the environmental good only by installing a threshold over which users must pass, but they do not restrict use after one has passed over that threshold, and the occasional users, in effect, subsidize the regular users.

TOWARD A THEORY OF ENVIRONMENTAL GOODS

Since environmental goods are both supplied and demanded, just as pecuniary goods, they can be subject to price analysis. Within the framework of Marshallian doctrine, there is a supply price associated with an environmental good which is equal to the minimum marginal cost of providing an additional unit of the good. There is also a demand price, which is the maximum amount buyers are willing and able to pay for an additional unit of the environmental good. The equilibrium price is found where the supply price and the demand price are equal. That equilibrium price is also associated with some equilibrium quantity of the environmental good, the quantity where the marginal cost of supply is just equal to the marginal social value of the good.

Application of economic analysis to environmental goods, particularly those of the coastal zone, requires that one be able to estimate with some degree of accuracy both the supply price and the demand price for any environmental good at various quantity levels. In the following chapters, we shall call on both Marshallian price theory and general equilibrium theory to derive quantitative tools for obtaining such estimates.

NOTES

1.   Anthony Scott, Natural Resources: The Economics of Conservation (Toronto: The University of Toronto Press, 1955), p. 10.

2.   Ibid., pp. 10-11.

3.   J. K. Galbraith, "How Much Should a Country Consume?" in Ian Burton and Robert W. Kates, eds., Readings in Resource Management and Conservation (Chicago: University of Chicago Press, 1965), p. 262.

4.   Scott, p. 11.

5.   Francis T. Christy and Anthony Scott, The Common Wealth in Ocean Fisheries: Some Problems of Growth and Economic Allocation (Baltimore: The Johns Hopkins Press, 1965), pp. 6-7.

6.   Ibid., p. 7.

7.   J. M. Stepp and H. H. Macaulay, The Pollution Problem (Washington, D.C.: American Enterprise Institute, 1968), p. 12.

8.   Ibid., p. 13.

9.   A. C. Pigou, The Economics of Welfare (4th ed.; London: Macmillan, 1960.)

10.   Ronald Coase, "The Problem of Social Cost," Journal of Law and Economics, October, 1960, pp. 1-44.

11.   M. Mason Gaffney, "Welfare Economics and the Environment," in Henry Jarrett, ed., Environmental Quality in a Growing Economy (Baltimore: The Johns Hopkins Press, 1966), p. 94.

12.   Coase, p. 2.

13.   James M. Buchanan, The Demand and Supply of Public Goods (Chicago: Rand McNally, 1968), pp. 77-97.

14. Ibid., p. 87.

15. See Buchanan, for example.

16. Paul Samuelson, "The Pure Theory of Public Expenditures," Review of Economics and Statistics, November, 1954, p. 387.

17. Buchanan, p. 11.

PART

II

A
CONCEPTUAL
FRAMEWORK

3

In the previous chapter, we developed an economic diagnosis of the problems of resource management in the coastal zone. In doing so, we noted that these problems arise largely out of the many useful attributes of the coastal zone which cannot be captured and placed on the market. We also noted that the side effects of man's activities in the coastal zone are often felt by parties other than the decision-maker, and, as a result, these side effects, or externalities, are not given adequate consideration in the market allocation of coastal zone resources.

In this chapter, we will develop a framework for analysis of coastal zone resources as they fit into an interrelated and complex economic system. To accomplish this task, we must formulate a conceptual framework for studying the linkages between the ecologic system and the socioeconomic system. Further, we must explore ways in which that conceptual framework can be manipulated for analysis of the problems related to environmental planning in the coastal zone.

THE RELEVANCE OF GENERAL
EQUILIBRIUM MODELS

Kenneth Boulding, in his famous "Spaceship Earth" article, has noted that mankind lives on earth in, essentially, what is a closed system.[1] With the exception of light energy received from the sun and heat radiated out into space, there are no new inputs into man's ecosystem nor are there new outputs. Instead, there is a materials cycle which involves man removing food, fuel, and other basic raw materials from the environment, processing those materials via a technology into more useful forms, and discarding the same materials back to the environment. The services of some goods are consumed, but the material substance of the goods themselves must ultimately be discharged in some form of waste.

Ayres and Kneese have taken the logical step beyond Boulding's "spaceship" presentation and have conceived of environmental pollution and its control as a materials balance problem for an entire economy. If the earth is virtually a closed system (in which there are no imports or exports), the weight of all the material residuals discharged back into the environment must be equal to the weight of the basic inputs entering the economic system. Some of these inputs are gaseous— e.g., oxygen taken from the atmosphere—and some of the residuals are also gaseous. Yet, if man uses materials from the natural environment, he must return the residuals of those materials to the environment. The questions are how they shall be returned and in what form. [2]

Most economists have approached the examination of environmental quality problems using partial equilibrium analysis. Air, water, and solid waste pollution have been viewed as separate problems. As Ayres and Kneese note, the partial equilibrium approach is both theoretically and empirically convenient, but it ignores the possibility of important trade-offs between the gaseous, liquid, or solid forms in which various material residuals may be discharged back into the environment. [3] Moreover, a partial equilibrium approach may result in a reduction in certain types of environmental pollution at the expense of increasing other types. For example, we can reduce water pollution by various types of treatment, but, in doing so, we create sludge which must either be burned or buried, thus creating air pollution or solid waste for disposal. Thus, comprehensive planning based on a series of partial equilibrium studies can be plagued by the fallacy of composition.

The existence of broad and complex interrelationships within an economic system has been appreciated by economic thinkers (if not very fully understood) since the time of François Quesnay, the French physiocrat of the eighteenth century who developed the Tableau economique. The reference point for most modern general equilibrium analysis, however, is found with another Frenchman, Leon Walras. Walras, who published his principal work in 1874, was interested in the simultaneous answers which an economic system gave to such questions as what is to be produced and how much is to be produced. He observed that these questions were not answered one at a time for each good or service, but simultaneously, in much the same way as a mathematician obtains a simultaneous solution to a set of algebraic equations. Thus, Walras constructed a general equilibrium model based on a series of simultaneous equations, each of which represented a good or service produced by the economy. It is the Walrasian general equilibrium model that Ayres and Kneese suggest as the "take-off point" for a meaningful analysis of regional environmental quality problems. [4]

INPUT-OUTPUT MODELS AS A GENERAL EQUILIBRIUM APPROACH

Walras considered his general equilibrium model as strictly a theoretical device. Both the data and the computational problems associated with the empirical implementation of such a model seemed almost insurmountable to him. By the 1930's, however, Professor Wassily Leontief had developed a theory of production based on the general equilibrium concept of economic interdependence. But Leontief went a step beyond theory and gave general equilibrium analysis an empirical tool when he published an input-output table for the United States economy in 1936. [5]

The essential structure of the Leontief input-output system is really very simple. [6] Table 1 shows the basic elements of a Leontief input-output table. Each row in the table accounts for the sales of the industry designated at the left. That is, Industry A sells $10 worth of goods to other firms in Industry A, $15 worth to firms in Industry B, $1 worth to firms in Industry C, and so on. Each column in the table accounts for the purchases of the industry designated across the top, so that Industry A purchases $10 worth of goods from other firms in Industry A, $5 worth from firms in Industry B, etc.

Within the Leontief system, goods are viewed as being purchased either for final consumption—i.e., goods going to "final demand"—or for intermediate use in producing other products within the processing sector. Suppose, for example, that Industry A in Table 1 is agriculture. We might envision some of agriculture's output, such as the leather made from cow's hides, being an intermediate point, and other agricultural output, such as beef, being a consumer's good. The Leontief table also shows purchases of imports, inventory, depletion, and depreciation as well as inventory accumulation, sales for export, and gross private capital formulation.

TABLE 1

Hypothetical Leontief Input-Output Table

Inputs \ Outputs		A	B	C	.....	N	Gross Inventory Accumulations	Exports	Gross Private Capital Formation	Households	Total Gross Output
Processing Sector	A	10	15	1	.....	6	2	5	3		64
	B	5	4	7	.....	8	1	6	3		59
	C	7	2	8	.....	3	1	1	2		40
	. . .					. . .					. . .
	N	2	6	7	.....	6	2	4	2		46
Payments Sector	Gross inventory depletion	1	2	0	.....	1					8
	Imports	2	1	3	.....	0					13
	Depreciation	1	2	1	.....	1					5
	Households										
	Total Gross Outlays	64	59	40	.....	46					450

The Leontief system can be completely closed, as Boulding's "spaceship earth," or it can be very open. In a closed Leontief table, all elements are endogenous—there are no imports or exports, and households are considered a part of the processing sector. If the table is very open, however, imports and exports will be excluded from the processing sector, as well as such semiautonomous factors as households and governmental activities.

The general equilibrium approach suggested by Ayres and Kneese views a materials flow from the environment into the processing and final demand sectors of the economy and, thence, back into the environment. Conceived within the framework of the Leontief system, this materials flow can be seen as a special type of import-export activity or intersystem trading between the ecosystem and the socio-economic system. Thus, by disaggregating the import and export sectors into various national resource components or types of material residuals, we can expand the Leontief input-output system into a general equilibrium model of economic-ecologic linkages in the coastal zone.

THE ISARD MODEL OF
ECONOMIC-ECOLOGIC LINKAGES

Professor Walter Isard, who has made innumerable contributions to the methods of regional planning, worked with Leontief in adapting the input-output system to analysis of open economics in areas such as subnational regions. His work in developing quantitative tools within a general equilibrium framework for evaluation of economic-ecologic linkages was independent of, but closely parallel to, the work of Ayres and Kneese.

The Isard model for analyzing ecologic-economic linkages is a linear system utilizing the concept of input-output models. Figure 1 graphically illustrates how the model might work. In the upper left-hand corner is a standard interindustry input-output matrix which shows the purchases (or sales) between industrial sectors associated with the production of one dollar's worth of gross output by each sector. Isard labels the data contained in this matrix "intersector coefficients." At the lower right-hand corner of the figure is a parallel matrix relating to the ecologic system. In this latter matrix are what Isard calls "interprocess coefficients." Finally, the over-all model is completed by two linkages matrixes. In the upper right-hand corner, Isard shows the exports of the socioeconomic system to the various segments of the ecosystem, and, in the lower left-hand

FIGURE 1

Schematic Representation of the
Isard Economic-Ecologic Models

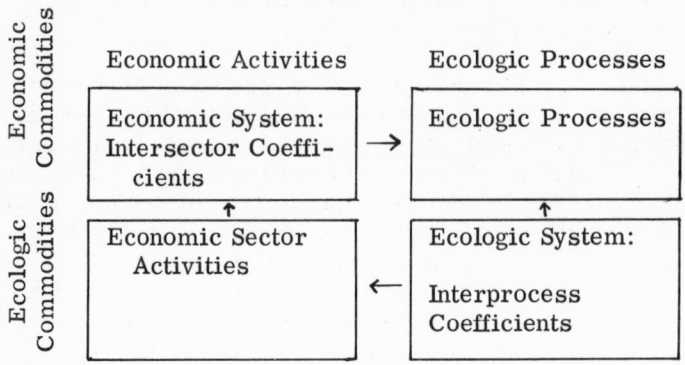

corner, he shows the imports from the ecosystem into the various
sectors of the interindustry matrix.[7]

The Isard model was developed in a highly disaggregate form.
The types of ecologic imports into the socioeconomic system are
specified in some detail. For example, in the Plymouth-Kingston-
Duxbury Bay case study, Isard attempts to identify the elements of
the food chain for winter flounder, specifying annelida, mollusca,
crustacea, etc., as inputs into the commercial fisheries sector.[8]
The all-encompassing nature of the model makes it difficult to avoid
this extreme disaggregation since the model attempts to describe the
very complex interprocesses of the ecologic system. As a result,
the Isard model requires enormous amounts of quantitative data, some
of which cannot now be obtained given the present status of ecologic
science. In his application of the model to planning problems in the
Plymouth-Kingston-Duxbury Bay area, Isard attempts to simplify
the model somewhat by eliminating sectors which do not seem relevant
to the particular problems at hand. In other cases, data are simply
assumed. The result is that the capability of the model for mathematical manipulation, in ways often associated with the input-output
framework, is restricted.

One other criticism can be leveled at the Isard model (as at all
input-output-type models). The relationships described in the model
are linear; all coefficients are assumed to be constant, regardless

of the scale. That is, we assume that the same amount of inputs are
required to produce the first pound of winter flounder as the fifth
pound, or the tenth pound. There are ecologic relationships which do
not exhibit linear characteristics. For example, the waterfowl that
migrate in large numbers will not decrease proportionately with
decreases of marshes and coastal waters; they require large areas of
marsh and coastal waters to exist at all. Professor Isard is aware of
the problems introduced by the constant coefficients required in a
linear input-output system, and he attempts to minimize these problems
by excluding processes from the structural input-output matrix that
seem not to use inputs in a linear way. These processes are then
considered separately in the Plymouth-Kingston-Duxbury study.[9]
While consideration of nonlinear processes outside the input-output
framework may be necessary, it is an admission of weakness in the
model by Isard himself. Moreover, it severely restricts the capa-
bilities of the model as a device for general equilibrium analysis.

A MODIFIED MODEL

Many of the problems of the Isard model appear to stem from
its all-encompassing nature. Ecologic inputs into the socioeconomic
system and socioeconomic outputs into the ecologic system can be
viewed at many different levels of aggregation. For example, we
can think of inputs as beach, hard marsh, soft marsh, and fast
ground, or we can lump all such inputs together as simply "land. "
The level of aggregation can be determined by the particular problem
at hand. If one attempts to construct such a universal model as that
proposed by Isard, however, he will probably be forced to go to considerable detail in specifying the exports from both the ecologic
and economic systems, mainly because of the enormous complexity
of the ecologic interprocesses. The achievement of our objective—
the identification of ecologic-economic linkages—does not require
such a comprehensive model, however. We are interested only in
the junctures of the socioeconomic and ecologic systems, and we
shall leave the ecologic interprocesses to more competent professionals
who study these processes. Consequently, we shall explore a modified
version of the Isard model as a method of achieving our somewhat
limited objective.

Figure 2 graphically illustrates a modified version of the Isard
model. The model is almost identical to the Isard model except for
the exclusion of the ecologic interprocess matrix in the right-hand
corner. In the upper left-hand corner is the same type of interindustry
input-output matrix used by Isard. It assumes a linear system and

FIGURE 2

Graphic Representation of a Modified Isard
Economic-Ecologic Model

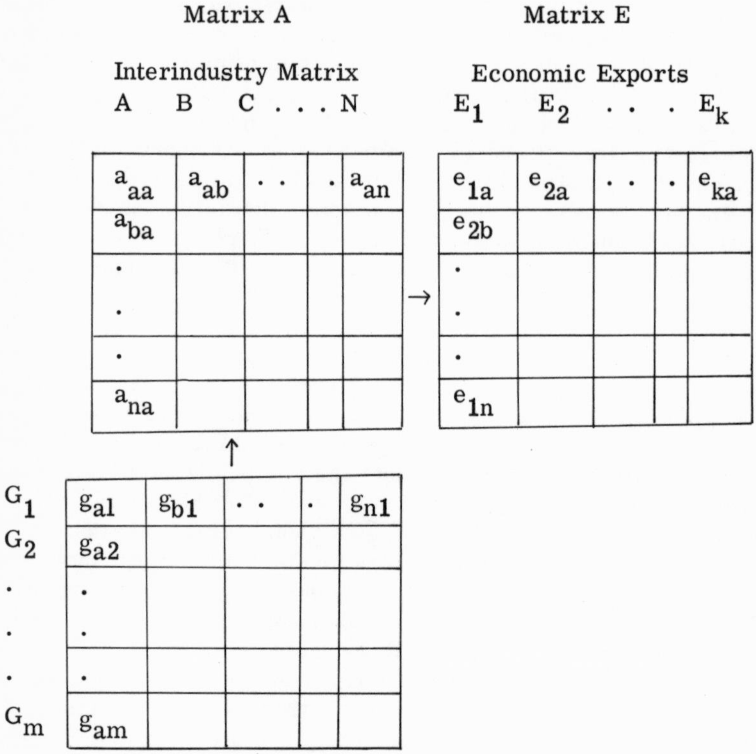

Matrix A   Matrix E

Interindustry Matrix   Economic Exports
A   B   C . . . N E_1 E_2 . .   . E_k

a_{aa}	a_{ab}	· ·	·	a_{an}
a_{ba}				
·				
·				
·				
a_{na}				

$\rightarrow$

e_{1a}	e_{2a}	· ·	·	e_{ka}
e_{2b}				
·				
·				
·				
e_{1n}				

$\uparrow$

G_1	g_{al}	g_{b1}	· ·	·	g_{n1}
G_2	g_{a2}				
·	·				
·	·				
·	·				
G_m	g_{am}				

constant coefficients. Each cell contains the amount (measured in
dollar values) of the output of the row industries required to produce
one dollar's worth of gross output by the industry heading the column.
Thus, a_{aa} is the amount of output of A required to produce one dollar
of gross output by A, a_{ba} is the amount of output of B required to
produce one dollar of gross output of A, and so on. We have labeled
this interindustry matrix the A matrix. Below the A matrix, in the
lower left-hand corner is the G matrix. It shows the amount of various
types of imports from the ecologic system required to produce one
dollar's worth of gross output by the industrial sectors in the A matrix.
That is, if G_1 is land, then g_{al} is the amount of land required to

produce one dollar of gross output by A, g_{b1}, the amount required to produce one dollar of gross output by B, etc. The E matrix, located in the upper right-hand corner, is analogous to the G matrix, except that it shows exports to the environment from the various industries in the A matrix.

The operational advantages of the modified model relate to the size of the G and E matrixes. We can have n number of industrial sectors in the A matrix, m number of environmental imports in the G matrix, and k number of environmental exports in the E matrix. These numbers are not constrained (or expanded) by an ecologic inter-process matrix as proposed by Isard. Hence, we can specify the ecologic-economic linkages at any level of aggregation we desire.

One other important modification can be made in the Isard model. Suppose that instead of constructing an E matrix, showing exports of pollutants and other materials into the environment from the socio-economic system, we consider such exports as negative imports— that is, we include elements in the G matrix which represent such outputs as BOD, SO_2, suspended atmospheric particulates, etc., and give them a negative sign. The operational significance of such a modification may not be immediately apparent, but, as we shall see later, it does facilitate mathematical manipulation without any loss of information. We will call this new matrix G'.

The modifications suggested above do not eliminate the necessity of assuming linear processes (constant coefficients). Yet they do make that assumption somewhat more palatable. It appears more reasonable to assume that water use or BOD output will vary propor-tionately with industrial output, for example, than it does to assume that fish populations will vary with the dissolved oxygen of the waters. The elimination of the ecologic interprocess matrix makes assumptions of that latter type unnecessary. Nevertheless, the modified model is a linear system and subject to the usual limitations associated with such a system.

THE MODEL AS AN ANALYTICAL
DEVICE—MATHEMATICAL POSSIBILITIES

The modified model presented above can be useful as a descrip-tive tool for identifying ecologic-economic linkages, but it also has properties which allow it to be manipulated mathematically for pur-poses of detailed analysis and planning. To explore these possibilities, we will need to resort to some elementary matrix algebra. In order to keep the presentation relatively intelligible to the nonmathematician, however, we will refrain from extensive matrix notation in favor of a graphic (though somewhat more cumbersome) presentation. The reader familiar with the basic mathematical ideas associated with the Leontief input-output system will find the next few paragraphs old ground, but it seems useful to review the properties of the Leontief model before applying its central idea to the problem of ecologic-economic linkages.

The interindustry, or A matrix, developed in our model is a Leontief input-output table—that is, it is a table of direct coefficients which show the "first-round" effects of a change in output of one sector on all the other sectors from which it purchases supplies. If we postmultiply the ecologic linkages, or G' matrix, we will obtain the R matrix shown below:

$$
\begin{matrix} G' \end{matrix} \qquad \begin{matrix} A \end{matrix} \qquad \begin{matrix} R \end{matrix}
$$

$$
\begin{bmatrix} g'_{a1} & g'_{b1} & \cdots & g'_{n1} \\ & & \cdot & \\ g'_{a2} & & \cdot & \\ \cdot & & \cdot & \\ \cdot & & \cdot & \\ \cdot & & \cdot & \\ \cdot & & \cdot & \\ \cdot & & \cdot & \\ g'_{am} & \cdots\cdots & g'_{mn} \end{bmatrix}
\times
\begin{bmatrix} a_{aa} & a_{ab} & \cdots & a_{an} \\ & & \cdot & \\ a_{ba} & & \cdot & \\ \cdot & & \cdot & \\ \cdot & & \cdot & \\ \cdot & & \cdot & \\ \cdot & & \cdot & \\ \cdot & & \cdot & \\ a_{na} & \cdots\cdots & a_{nn} \end{bmatrix}
=
\begin{bmatrix} r_{a1} & r_{b1} & \cdots & r_{n1} \\ & & \cdot & \\ r_{a2} & & \cdot & \\ \cdot & & \cdot & \\ \cdot & & \cdot & \\ \cdot & & \cdot & \\ \cdot & & \cdot & \\ \cdot & & \cdot & \\ r_{am} & \cdots\cdots & r_{nm} \end{bmatrix}
$$

The elements of the resulting R matrix show the direct effects on the environment associated with one dollar's increase in final output by each sector A through N and for each environmental good 1 through M in the ecologic linkages matrix.

We can now turn to a more general solution using basically the same mathematics. If we subtract the A matrix from an identity matrix (a matrix in which all elements are zero except those on the northwest-southeast diagonal, those on the diagonal being one) and invert the results, we get what is called the Leontief inverse.[10] The significance of the Leontief inverse is that it provides a matrix of direct plus indirect requirements per \$1 of final demand for each sector in the system. Consequently, we obtain information not only on the "first-round" effects of an increase in sales to final demand by each sector, but also information on second, third, fourth, etc., round effects. Each entry in the Leontief inverse matrix shows the total dollar production directly and indirectly required by per dollar of final demand deliveries by the sector at the top of the column from the sectors at the left-hand side of the table. We will call the inverted matrix A'.

Now we can postmultiply our G' matrix by the A' matrix and obtain the direct and indirect environmental effects of one dollar's increase in delivery to final demand by each of the sectors in the inter-industry table. That is, since each row in the G' matrix shows the amount of a given environmental good for each dollar's worth of output by each sector and each column in the A' matrix shows the purchases of output required from each sector for the sector at the top to increase its deliveries to final demand by one dollar, the sum of the products of the elements of the G' row and the A' column gives us both the direct and indirect effects of a particular environmental good of one dollar's increase in final demand by each row in the A' matrix. Graphically, the matrix multiplication can be represented:

$$
\begin{array}{ccc}
G' & A' & R' \\[4pt]
\begin{bmatrix}
g'_{al} & g'_{bl} & \cdots & g'_{nl} \\
g'_{a2} & & & \\
\vdots & & & \\
& & & \\
& & & \\
& & & \\
g'_{am} & \cdots & & g'_{nm}
\end{bmatrix}
&
\times
\begin{bmatrix}
a'_{aa} & a'_{ab} & \cdots & a'_{an} \\
a'_{ba} & & & \\
\vdots & & & \\
& & & \\
& & & \\
& & & \\
a'_{na} & \cdots & & a'_{nn}
\end{bmatrix}
&
=
\begin{bmatrix}
r'_{al} & r'_{bl} & \cdots & r'_{nl} \\
r'_{a2} & & & \\
\vdots & & & \\
& & & \\
& & & \\
& & & \\
r'_{am} & \cdots & & r'_{nm}
\end{bmatrix}
\end{array}
$$

where the elements of the R' matrix are exactly analogous to the R matrix, except that they show the total environmental effects, both direct and indirect.

A HYPOTHETICAL EXAMPLE

Since the manipulation of matrixes above involve considerable abstract reasoning, possible application of the model may be clearer if we work through a simple example. As of this date, no empirical data for use in such a model are available, so hypothetical data will be used.

Assume we have an economy which can be described by three sectors, A, B, and C, so that the Leontief inverse, or A' matrix for this economy is:

$$
\begin{array}{c}
 & \begin{array}{ccc} A & B & C \end{array} \\
\begin{array}{c} A \\ B \\ C \end{array}
\begin{array}{|c|c|c|}
\hline 1 & 2 & 3 \\ \hline 1 & 3 & 3 \\ \hline 1 & 2 & 4 \\ \hline
\end{array}
\end{array}
\quad = \quad
\begin{bmatrix} 1 & 2 & 3 \\ 1 & 3 & 3 \\ 1 & 2 & 4 \end{bmatrix}
\quad = A'
$$

Assume we are interested in only two environmental goods, land use and BOD output, so that the G' matrix is:

$$
\begin{array}{c}
 & \begin{array}{ccc} A & B & C \end{array} \\
\begin{array}{c} \text{Land Use} \\ \text{(in acres)} \\ \text{BOD/lbs/} \\ \text{day} \end{array}
\begin{array}{|c|c|c|}
\hline 2 & 2 & 3 \\ \hline -1 & -3 & -2 \\ \hline
\end{array}
\end{array}
\quad = \quad
\begin{bmatrix} 2 & 2 & 3 \\ -1 & -3 & -2 \end{bmatrix}
\quad = G'
$$

And, postmultiplying G' times A', we get:

$$
\begin{bmatrix} 2 & 2 & 3 \\ -1 & -3 & -2 \end{bmatrix}
\begin{bmatrix} 1 & 2 & 3 \\ 1 & 3 & 3 \\ 1 & 2 & 4 \end{bmatrix}
=
\begin{bmatrix} 7 & 16 & 24 \\ -6 & -15 & -20 \end{bmatrix}
$$

The R' matrix can be relabeled as a table for interpretative purposes, so that:

Producing Industry	Total Use or Output Associated With $1 Delivery to Final Demand	
	Land Use (acres)	BOD/lbs/day
A	7	-6
B	16	-15
C	24	-20

From the table, we see that each $1 increase in final demand for industry A will result in the use of seven more acres of land and the additional release of six pounds per day of BOD. Similar information can be obtained for industry B and C. One can also obtain estimates of the total land use or BOD released by multiplying each of the elements in the table by the dollar value of final demand for each sector.

TOWARD AN EMPIRICAL MODEL

It should be intuitively apparent that even the modified model demonstrated above would require enormous amounts of empirical data if it is to be made operational and used as a planning tool. There are several data problems, however, in addition to the quantity of data required.

1. The coefficients in the ecologic linkages (G') matrix are very sensitive to the level of technology. The same final product can be produced, in many cases, by several alternative processes, and, ideally, one would desire coefficients for each possible process within the industrial sector.

2. The coefficients in the ecologic linkages (G') matrix are very sensitive to the level of aggregation of the industrial sectors. For example, the average BOD output for the entire food-processing industry may be very different than the average BOD for the diary-foods-processing segment of the food-processing industry.

3. The negative coefficients of the ecologic linkages (G') matrix can be specified as "before treatment," or "after treatment." If they are "before treatment" coefficients, they represent raw outputs and are relatively unambiguous. If they are "after treatment," we need to specify the level and type of treatment.

These three points are not, in and of themselves, related to the data-quantity problem, but they do imply that a really useful empirical model of ecologic-economic linkages must have several alternative sets of data.

APPLICATION TO ENVIRONMENTAL PLANNING

The modified general equilibrium model we have developed in this chapter can be a useful tool to planners concerned with a balance between economic development and ecologic viability of the coastal zone in at least four ways:

1. It provides a basis for examining the effects of future national

economic growth on the extraction of resources from the coastal zone and on inputs into the coastal zone environment.

2. It provides a framework for the analysis of the overall economic effects of zoning regulations which restrict certain types of resource usage.

3. It provides a similar framework for the analysis of the overall economic effects of various types and levels of emission standards which might be required of industries operating in the coastal zone.

4. Finally (and perhaps, most importantly), it allows the planning process to become an exercise in systems analysis, rather than an exercise in fragmental problem-solving, thus making possible coastal zone resource plans based on the concept of multiple-use management.

Useful as such a modified general equilibrium model may be, however, it cannot, in and of itself, answer all the questions which planners concerned with coastal zone management must answer. The model developed in this chapter can provide estimates of the opportunity costs associated with diverting coastal zone resources from pecuniary uses into environmental goods, but it cannot provide estimates of the value of those environmental goods. That is, the model is useful only in estimating the "supply price" of the environmental good—the minimum opportunity cost associated with making a specific quantity of a particular environmental good available to the users of that environmental good. The model, as constituted in this chapter, can tell us nothing about the "demand price", or the maximum sacrifice which users of environmental goods are willing to make in order to obtain the use of the environmental good. Without parallel knowledge of the demand price for environmental goods, we cannot derive an optimum allocation of coastal zone resources between environmental and pecuniary uses. In the next chapter, we will look at possible approaches to estimating such demand prices.

NOTES

1. K. E. Boulding, "The Economics of the Coming Spaceship Earth, " in Henry Jarett, ed., Environmental Quality in a Growing Economy (Baltimore: The Johns Hopkins Press, 1966), pp. 3-14.

2. Robert V. Ayres and Allen V. Kneese, "Production, Consumption, and Externalities," American Economic Review, LIX, 284-85.

3. Ibid., p. 295.

4. Ibid., p. 288.

5. William H. Miernyk, The Elements of Input-Output Analysis (New York: Random House, 1967), pp. 4-5. For Leontief's basic table, see his article, "Quantitative Input-Output Relations in the Economic System of the United States, " Review of Economics and Statistics, XXVIII, 105-25.

6. The following discussion draws heavily on Miernyk, pp. 8-29.

7. Walter Isard, "Some Notes on the Linkage of the Ecologic and Economic System," Regional Science Association Papers, XXII (1969), 86-87.

8. Walter Isard and others, "Ecologic-Economic Analysis for Regional Development, " Regional Science and Landscape Analysis Project, Graduate School of Design, Harvard University, Cambridge, Mass., December, 1968, pp. 502-3.

9. Ibid., p. 174.

10. For a detailed but short explanation, see William H. Miernyk, The Elements of Input-Output Analysis (New York: Random House, 1965), pp. 128-51.

4

ENVIRONMENTAL GOODS
AS
ECONOMIC
COMMODITIES

In closing Chapter 3, we noted that it was not enough to know the supply prices associated with the environmental good of the coastal zone. If we are to manage the resources of the coastal zone wisely and allocate those scarce resources between competing environmental and pecuniary uses, we must also know the demand prices associated with environmental goods. Our objective in this chapter is to develop the concept of environmental goods as economic commodities and to explore ways of estimating the demand prices of environmental goods of the coastal zone.

ENVIRONMENTAL GOODS AND THE GENERAL THEORY OF DEMAND

Although there are no explicit markets for environmental goods and, consequently, no explicit prices placed on these goods, one can still conceive of these goods having a demand price based on maximum willingness to pay to enjoy the flow of services that are associated with such things as clean air, clean water, beautiful beaches, and open marshes. We know from experience that such environmental goods are desired by the public and that the public is willing to make some sacrifice to obtain these goods. For example, residents of the continental interior may and do incur considerable travel expenses, both in time and money, to visit coastal areas and enjoy their beaches during vacation. The question is: How intense is this desire for environmental goods; how much of a sacrifice are persons willing to make? The answer to that question will give us an estimate of the demand prices for environmental goods.

In Chapter 2, we divided all goods into one of two classes—pecuniary goods and environmental goods. Pecuniary goods were defined as those that are marketable in some way, those which have an explicit price attached to them as they flow through the commercial sectors of our economy. Environmental goods were defined as nonmarketable services of natural resources. For the present, let us not be concerned about the heterogeneous nature of pecuniary goods or environmental goods. Instead, let us imagine a situation in which an individual is faced with a choice of having either pecuniary goods, environmental goods, or some combination of the two. How can economic theory help us to analyze this situation?

The economist has a tool readily adaptable to analysis of choice between two types of commodities. It is called an indifference map, and an example is shown in Figure 3. Every individual has such a map, although he is not likely to be conscious of it—that is, each individual has a variety of combinations of pecuniary goods and environmental goods which will give him equal utility or satisfaction. Using Figure 3, suppose that the individual is equally satisfied if he has OA amount to environmental goods and OB amount of pecuniary goods, or if he has OA' amount of environmental goods and OB' amount of pecuniary goods. He remains indifferently between the two combinations, or between any combinations that lie on line $1_1 1_1'$. Of course, the individual might like to have more of both types of commodities; i.e., he would like to move from line $1_1 1_1'$ to line $1_2 1_2'$ or to line $1_3 1_3'$. Yet, along any of those lines, he is indifferent to the combination of environmental and pecuniary goods. Each individual will have a different indifference map on which the shape of the indifference lines will vary according to the individual's taste and preferences. The indifference map is very abstract, subjective, and personal, but it can be used to conceive of how an individual might substitute one type of goods for another without any net change in satisfaction or well-being (as the individual judges his own well-being).

There is an implicit assumption in the indifference map as shown in Figure 3 that additional environmental goods can be obtained only by giving up some pecuniary goods, and vice versa. Later we will attempt to support that assumption, but, if we accept it for the present, we can use the indifference map to place a value on the environmental goods in terms of the pecuniary goods—that is, it can be argued that, since there is no change in the net satisfaction of the individual as he moves toward the left along any given indifference line, the additional environmental goods he obtained must be just equal in value to the pecuniary goods he has given up. So, if the individual feels no change in satisfaction, either positively or negatively, when he gives up, say,

FIGURE 3

Hypothetical Indifference Map for
Environmental and Pecuniary Goods

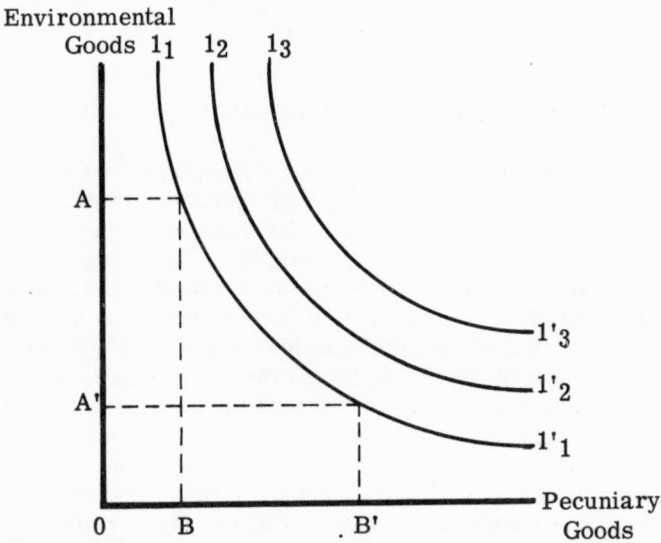

$10 worth of pecuniary goods and obtains one unit more of clean air,
that unit of clean air must be valued by that individual at $10. Thus,
given that the pecuniary goods can be measured in dollar terms, it is
possible to translate the environmental goods to dollar terms by ob-
serving the rate of substitution along any indifference line. The dollar
value of any unit of environmental good is the slope of the indifference
line.

When we move to a lower level of abstraction, the indifference
map analysis becomes much more difficult. One cannot easily aggregate all environmental goods into one lump. How do we aggregate,
for example, clean air and clean water? To what common units can
the two be converted, and, even if such common units are found, are
the two types of environmental goods independent of one another so
that the satisfaction one realized from them is the sum total of the
units of clean air and clean water available? Although one can show

abstractly how indifference maps might be used to estimate the economic value of environmental goods, the maps are not very helpful as operational devices. Still they point the way to such estimation by showing that the economic value of an environmental good is identical to the value of the pecuniary goods which individuals are willing to give up to obtain them. Thus, if we wish to accomplish the objective of assigning economic values to certain nonmarket environmental goods, we must determine the value of the pecuniary goods which individuals are willing to give up to obtain them.

THE QUANTITY OF ENVIRONMENTAL GOODS

Natural resources, such as clean air and clean water, are not unlimited, even in the absence of human polluting activities. For example, at any time and under any given atmospheric or hydrologic conditions, there is only so much clean air or clean water available in a region. Human society seeks to make use of this limited supply of air and water in two ways: (1) they seek clean air and water to be consumed (as they are) as environmental goods, e.g., by breathing, viewing, etc.; and (2) they seek to use the air and water resources in the production of pecuniary goods with the result of changing their form by the introduction of materials we call pollutants. The use of air and water to produce pecuniary goods reduces the quantity of clean air and clean water available for consumption as environmental goods unless the air and water are treated in some way to remove the polluting materials before release back into the environment. Since this treatment requires installation of additional equipment and processes, it increases the monetary costs of producing pecuniary goods and reduces the quantity available at any given budget level. Hence, the use of clean air and clean water as environmental goods reduces the quantity of pecuniary goods available to individuals with a given budget of total expendable money available. Thus, the implicit assumption made with regard to the indifference map analysis above is seen to be realistic: Additional environmental goods can be obtained only by giving up some pecuniary goods, and additional pecuniary goods can be obtained only by giving up some environmental goods. The sole qualification to this assumption is that we are operating on a fixed budget (which is likely to be true over any short period of time).

SOME RELEVANT HYPOTHESES

The conceptual framework developed above shows that the value of any particular environmental good is equal to the value of the pecuniary goods which individuals are willing to forego in order to obtain it. That statement does not imply, however, that the value of an environmental good is constant over all quality levels or all individuals. In this section, we shall turn our attention to the factors which may serve as sources of variation in the amount individuals are willing to pay for any given environmental good. We shall attempt to reach, a priori, some logical hypotheses about such variation in the willingness to pay for the two environmental goods, clean air and clean water.

Quality Levels

Air or water can be consumed at many different quality levels as an environmental good. For example, one can consume air which has no odor, but which may pose a threat to health, or one can consume very high quality air which both has no odor and possesses no possible threat to health. It seems reasonable to argue that the amount of pecuniary goods individuals are willing to forego for clean air or clean water is positively related to just how clean that air or water is. But how do we measure the cleanliness of air or water? One way, of course, is to use various engineering standards and to hypothesize that the amount individuals are willing to pay for clean air or clean water increases directly with improvements in air or water quality as measured against these standards. That is, willingness to pay increases with reduction in the concentration of suspended particles, or sulfur oxides, in the air and with the amount of dissolved oxygen in the water. Use of these engineering standards of environmental quality presumes that the layman perceives of quality in the same way as the environmental scientist. Since the average layman is probably unaware of what various technical standards mean to him in terms of odor or health, however, it is doubtful that the technological ordering of air or water quality will coincide exactly with the layman's perception of quality. After all, environmental quality is a subjective concept subject to influence of the peculiar experiences of each individual. Yet, in the absence of a priori evidence to the contrary, we are left with only the engineering standards of quality for our hypothesis, which we state formally as:

Hypothesis I: The percentage of gross annual income which households are willing to forego for air or water quality is positively related to the level of air or water quality being obtained, such level of quality being measured by common engineering standards.

Residence Zone

Another source of variation in the amount individuals are willing to pay for air or water quality is the individual's experience with the environment. Willingness to forego pecuniary goods in order to achieve clean air and/or clean water is dependent upon the individual's awareness of environmental alternatives. Thus, an individual who has lived all his life in an environment which is characterized by an abundance of clean air and clean water may tend to take these environmental goods for granted, not fully comprehending the problems associated with pollution of the environment. By the same token, an individual who has never experienced clean air and/or clean water may be so adjusted to the pollution that he cannot fully comprehend the value of a clean environment. In a relatively small region, such as a single metropolitan area, however, where a broad spectrum of air and water qualities are available, an individual is likely to have experienced both clean air and water and polluted air and water. This latter individual, therefore, is aware, within some range, of the environmental alternatives which are open. If within this relatively small region, such factors of the social environment as school quality, police and fire protection, etc., are more or less constant, we can expect the individual to seek a residence zone of the highest quality environment he can find, given his budget constraint. It follows, hence, that, other things being constant, the residents of relatively clean air and/or water zones are likely to place a higher value, in terms of willingness to pay, on these environmental goods than will residents (especially long-term residents) of polluted zones. As Ridker observes,[1]

> In the case of the asthma victim who stays in the polluted area, we must assume that he knows what he is doing, i.e., that for him it is cheaper to stay than to move (perhaps because of the psychic costs involved in moving). While this is equivalent to assuming rational and knowledgeable behavior, any other assumption would require us to look into the mind of each affected person.

On the basis of this a priori reasoning, we can formulate a second hypothesis:

Hypothesis II: In a region of mixed environmental quality, the percentage of gross annual income which households are willing to forego for air and water quality is higher in relatively clean zones than in relatively polluted zones.

Income Levels

A likely third source of variation in the amount individuals are willing to pay for environmental quality is income level. Pecuniary goods are often assumed to have diminishing marginal utility, i.e., an additional dollar to a millionaire is not likely to produce as much satisfaction as an additional dollar to a pauper. A low-income family may be hard-pressed to meet the bare necessities of pecuniary goods— food, clothing, and shelter—and, thus, will find it a greater sacrifice to forego these pecuniary goods for environmental quality than the high-income family. Professor Mason Gaffney has made this point in suggesting that air and water quality are "superior goods," i.e., individuals are willing to allocate a greater and greater percentage of their incomes to obtain environmental goods as their incomes rise.[2] A priori, therefore, it seems reasonable to formulate a third hypothesis which can be stated thus:

Hypothesis III: The percentage of gross annual household income which households are willing to forego for air and water quality is positively related to the income level of the households.

Interaction of Income and Residence Zone

The last two sources of variation in willingness to pay for air and water quality which are hypothesized above are not independent of one another. We might well expect the residences of higher-income families to be concentrated geographically in the relatively clean zones. The higher the household income, the less constraining the budget factor in the residence location decision. Hence, if individuals choose to live in the best environment they can afford, the higher the income, the better the environment. Household income levels and environmental quality of the residence zone are, therefore, likely to be interrelated. For purposes of isolating the effect of each factor as a source of variation in willingness to pay, we might formulate a fourth (somewhat supplementary) hypothesis:

Hypothesis IV: The percentage of gross annual household income which households are willing to forego for air or water quality is positively affected by the interaction between household income levels and environmental quality in the residence zone of the household.

AN ANALYTICAL MODEL—GENERAL MODEL

The hypotheses formulated above need to be restated in order to subject them to statistical testing. We can proceed to do this by development of a linear model. Let there be n different quantity levels, m different household income levels, and two levels of environmental quality in residence zones (clean or dirty). Then, we can develop a model of the form:

$$Y_{ijk} = \mu + \rho_i + \alpha_j + \delta_k + (\alpha \delta)_{jk} + \epsilon_{ijk}$$

where

Y_{ijk} = the percentage of gross annual household income which a household of income level j, living in a residence zone of environmental quality k, is willing to forego for quality level i of an environmental good;

μ = a constant;

ρ_i = the effect of quantity i on willingness to pay;

α_j = the effect of income level j, on willingness to pay;

δ_k = the effect of environmental quality k in the residence zone;

$(\alpha \delta)_{jk}$ = the effect of the interaction between income levels and environmental quality in the residence zone on willingness to pay;

ϵ_{ijk} = a random error term.

Conceived as an analysis of variance model, the various factors of quality levels, income levels, zone of residence, and zone-income interaction can be viewed as sources of variation around some mean willingness to pay represented by the constant (μ). Using the notation of the model to restate the hypotheses in a null format suitable for statistical testing, we get:

Hypothesis I: ρ_i = 0, all i

Hypothesis II: δ_k = 0, all k

Hypothesis III: α_j = 0, all j

Hypothesis IV: $(\alpha \delta)_{jk}$ = 0, all j, all k

DATA NEEDS

Statistical tests of these null hypotheses, using empirical data, can be performed if we can obtain observations on willingness to pay for each quality level and income level split by each of two residential zones (say, a clean zone and a polluted zone). The tests are conducted by calculating the reduction in the total sum of the squared deviations from the mean accounted for by each of the hypothesized sources of variation. Basically, the problem resolves itself into a split-plot analysis of variance design.[3] To perform the statistical tests, however, we must have data on the willingness of individual households to pay for various levels of air and water quality. We must also have data on annual income and on environmental quality in the zone of residence of the household observed.

Since, by definition, environmental goods are not purchased in the marketplace, information on willingness to pay cannot be obtained directly from observable prices. Allen Kneese, Mason Gaffney, and others have argued that land rents and the land values capitalized from these rents are proxy measures of willingness to pay for particular levels of environmental quality.[4] Indeed, a study by Professor Hugh O. Nourse of the effect of air pollution on house values in St. Louis showed that unit property values tended to increase by $245 for every .5 milligram decrease in sulphur trioxide per 100 square centimeters per day, ceteris paribus.[5] Several studies of the effect of air pollution on property values have been conducted under the direction of Professor Thomas D. Crocker.[6] Studies of residential property values by Crocker and colleagues in St. Louis, Kansas City and Washington, D.C., indicate that the offer price on owner-occupied housing decreases by $300 to $700 per property unit with an increase of one unit in a "composite" pollution index including both particulates and sulfides.

Another approach to willingness-to-pay data is a household survey which questions individuals about their attitudes toward environmental quality and their willingness to pay to obtain it. Ridker attempted to use this latter approach with somewhat unsatisfactory results in ascertaining the psychic cost of air pollution.[7] More successfull attempts were made by Davis in a study of the value of outdoor recreation[8] and by Frederickson and Magnas in a study of attitudes toward water pollution in Syracuse.[9]

Undoubtedly, most economists would prefer to measure willingness to pay using capitalized land values. Such a measurement is based on actual payment and, consequently, can be accepted as response in a real, rather than hypothetical situation. Yet a purchase of residential property involves acquisition of a whole bundle of assets (and liabilities)—the land, a house, location relative to shopping centers, schools, neighbors, and many more. While there are econometric devices to allow separation of the effect of some of these factors on the property value, these devices do not perform perfectly. Moreover, a newcomer to a particular city may purchase residential property without being fully aware of the level of environmental pollution prevailing at that site. Consequently, relative differences in the value of similar property in polluted versus unpolluted areas is only an approximation of the willingness to pay for environmental quality. More importantly, perhaps, property values are not apt to be affected at all by willingness to pay to obtain such environmental goods as marshland and beaches.

The alternative approach to obtaining willingness-to-pay data is not very attractive either. Household surveys, even with the use of highly sophisticated questionnaires and well-trained enumerators, run the risk that the interviewee would not respond in a real situation in the same way he responds in the hypothetical situation posed by the enumerator. The respondent may reason that talk is cheap and exaggerate his answers about willingness to pay in the belief that he will never really have to lay his money on the line. Or, on the other extreme, the respondent may be suspicious that his answer will be used to justify an actual charge (in the form of taxes or higher prices) and understate his true willingness to pay. A priori, there is no way to determine the direction of the bias in the response to the survey. Indeed, some respondents may be subject to one bias, some to the other. Add to these perfectly understandable biases the difficulties of phrasing questions that can be understood and interpreted properly by the respondent and one can begin to appreciate the limitations associated with a household survey on willingness to pay.[10] While the household-survey approach has the advantage of being straightforward, only repeated use of the survey, with tests of the results against estimates based on capitalized-property-value differential and survey results from similar samples in many localities, will determine if the technique can be used with confidence to obtain data for simulating the demand for environmental goods.

USE OF WILLINGNESS-TO-PAY ESTIMATES IN PLANNING

Theoretical economists find the notion of the equilibrium a peculiarly entrancing idea. Equilibrium in the market is obtained when the supply price is equal to the demand price. At that point, the minimum amount sellers are willing to accept for a commodity is just equal to the maximum amount buyers are willing to pay, and at that point, in a free market, an optimum allocation of resources is achieved. In Chapter 3, we developed a framework for ascertaining the supply price and, in this chapter, we have suggested an approach to ascertaining demand price. Hence, if we synthesize the two chapters, we should be able to develop a procedure for finding the optimum allocation of the natural resources of the coastal zone between pecuniary and environmental uses.

Unfortunately, such environmental goods as clean air or clean water cannot be purchased in small increments. Either a community has air which has no odor or it does not. Willingness to pay for non-odorous air, therefore, must be evaluated in terms of the actual cost of obtaining that environmental good. If the aggregate sum of the community's willingness to pay is equal to, or greater than, the actual, or opportunity, cost, the planner can obtain a clear-cut answer using the conceptual tools we have forged in these chapters. If the aggregate sum of the community's willingness to pay is less than the actual, or opportunity, cost, the planner faces an ambiguous situation in which an easy solution is not available.

Perhaps we can better grasp the limitations of our tools if we illustrate with a hypothetical situation. Suppose a new plant desires to locate in a community and that we find, using the modified model in Chapter 3, it will add $10 million per year, directly and indirectly, to the community's income but, at the same time, also emit gaseous waste which will cause an unpleasant odor in the air. Suppose also that we have found the community is willing to forego up to $6 million annually in income to avoid odor in the air. Superficially, we might note that the community is not willing to sacrifice enough to avoid the odor to merit keeping the plant out of the community. But, if we made our decision on such superficial inspection, we might overlook a better solution. For example, what if the plant could install equipment which would eliminate the odor for $5 million per year? Even if the entire cost of that equipment came out of the income which would have accrued to the community (rather than, say, to nonlocal stockholders), the community would clearly be better off. There would be no odor and the net income of the community would increase by $5 million per year.

Still, there are other problems associated with this analysis of which one ought, at least, to be conscious. Who bears the cost of avoiding odor, for example? The $5 million required annually in the example above to abate odor might be borne by the community, but what segment of the community? We have explicitly considered in this chapter that some segments of the community might be willing to pay a greater amount for environmental quality than others. The development of institutional arrangements for seeing that those most willing to pay do in fact pay the greater share is not an easy task. It involves the entire tax structure of a community and of the nation. As such, it is a can of worms best left unopened in this study. But it must not be left unopened forever, because rational resource management to obtain environmental quality will require that it be examined in some detail.

NOTES

1. Ronald G. Ridker, Economic Costs of Air Pollution: Studies in Measurement (New York: Praeger, 1967), p. 10.

2. M. Mason Gaffney, "Welfare Economics and the Environment," Henry Jarrett, ed., Environmental Quality in a Growing Economy (Baltimore: The Johns Hopkins Press, 1966), p. 91.

3. See Robert G. D. Steel and James H. Torrie, Principles and Procedures of Statistics (New York: McGraw-Hill, 1960), pp. 252-57.

4. Gaffney, p. 89.

5. Hugh O. Nourse, "The Effect of Air Pollution on House Values," Land Economics, XLIII (May, 1967), 187.

6. See R. J. Anderson, Jr., and T.D. Crocker, "Air Pollution and Housing: Some Findings," Paper No. 264, Institute for Research in the Behavioral, Economic, and Management Sciences, Krannert Graduate School of Industrial Management, Purdue University, Lafayette, December, 1969; and T. D. Crocker, Some Economic Aspects of Air Pollution Control with Special Reference to Polk County, Florida, Report to the U.S. Public Health Service, January, 1968.

7. Ridker, p. 19.

8.   Robert K. Davis, "The Value of Outdoor Recreation: An Economic Study of the Maine Woods," Ph. D. thesis, Harvard University, Cambridge, Mass. , 1963, pp. 18-37.

9.   H. George Frederickson and Howard Magnas, "Comparing Attitudes Toward Water Pollution in Syracuse," Water Resources Research, IV (October, 1968), 877-89.

10.   See Ridker, p. 19, for his enumeration of the limitations of a household-survey approach.

As discussed in Chapter 2, the application of economic analysis to environmental resources, particularly those of the coastal zone, requires that one be able to estimate with some degree of accuracy both the supply price and demand price for any environmental good at various quantity levels. Chapters 6, 7, and 8 are a report on the efforts to implement empirically a model, such as we have described in earlier chapters, for the Charleston, South Carolina, metropolitan area.

THE STUDY AREA

For purposes of this case study, the Charleston metropolitan area was defined as Charleston, Berkeley, and Dorchester counties. These counties are located near the center of the coastal zone of South Carolina and in the South Atlantic area of the Atlantic Coast. The counties are closely allied economically, socially, and politically, with the port city of Charleston providing the primary urban focus. The close ties between the three counties are evidenced by the fact that the three counties have a central planning agency and a single chamber of commerce. Charleston is a peninsula city bounded by the Ashley and Cooper Rivers; however, the urban area has spread across both rivers as well as inland along major transportation routes. The two rivers converge to form Charleston harbor and to create an estuarine environment with extensive marshland.

Altogether, the Charleston study area consists of 2,614 square miles (approximately the geographic size of Delaware), and the preliminary results of the 1970 census placed the population at 316,339, about 60 percent of which is estimated to be urban. The total work force in 1967 was 112,530, with approximately 4 percent unemployed. Approximately 35 percent of the population participate in the work force. In 2969, 29 percent or 26,680 of the households in the area had incomes of less than $3,000.

The Charleston Standard Metropolitan Statistical Area (SMSA) has a number of advantages that make it suited for applying the model developed in Chapter 3. These are as follows:

1. The area is not too large, either in population or business activities, to permit the collection of primary data within the cost and time limitations.

2. Though the area is not too large, it still presents a diversified industrial base, contains a number of extractive activities, and has a large potential for development of recreational opportunities.

3. The area is beginning to experience strong conflicts between the various activities utilizing the coastal zone. Due to a large number of activities using the area, many of the conflicts arising are representative of problems taking place all along the Atlantic and Gulf coasts.

THE CHARLESTON ECONOMY AND
THE COASTAL ZONE

The resources of the coastal zone form an important element of the economic base for the Charleston area. Charleston Harbor pervades the entire economic structure of the area. Charleston, as a port, ranks thirteenth in the nation in value of foreign commerce. There are at least twelve large naval facilities located in the area as a direct result of the harbor. The area also draws a relatively large tourist trade due to harbor-related attractions such as Fort Sumter and Fort Moultrie, as well as to other historic attractions. The intercoastal waterway traverses the entire sixty-mile length of the area's coastline and provides some economic impact on its own.

Unfortunately, the Charleston Harbor picture is not all pleasant. The harbor has a definite silting problem which results in almost continuous dredging operations. The result of this dredging is that thousands of acres of once productive salt marsh have been diked and utilized as spoil areas. In fact, so many acres have been utilized for spoil disposal that there are very few areas left for disposal in the future. Pollution, in terms of industrial wastes, insecticides and pesticides, and raw sewage, also constitutes a problem area. Due to the present conditions in the harbor, polluting materials discharged into the water are not flushed out of the system, but are "trapped" in the harbor. In addition, many of the industrial concerns located in the area which utilize the port facilities contribute large amounts of air pollution.

Moreover, while the study area has been heavily impacted by military installations, the Charleston area remains one of chronic low income. In 1968, the Charleston metropolitan area ranked as the sixth lowest SMSA in the nation in per capita income.[1] Local planners and developers are in general agreement that the Charleston area must diversify its economy, but it must do so in such a way as to minimize further environmental degradation and preserve the delicate ecologic balance of the coastal zone in which it is located.

ORGANIZATION OF THE CASE STUDY

Chapter 6 involves the construction of an economic input-output model for a coastal area on the basis of a field survey. To the present, most of the regional studies involving input-output analysis have dealt with regions around large urban centers or with large multistate regions such as Appalachia. When such studies have dealt with small local regions, they have often had primary purposes such as evaluating water-based recreation or some other specific objective. As a result, little is known about small local economies, and this is especially true for local economies that are directly tied to a coastal environment. It is hoped that the model built in Chapter 5 will provide information about the functioning of small coastal economies as well as providing the economic part of the modified model discussed in Chapter 3.

Chapter 7 reports the building of an ecologic matrix to complete the modified enviromental good model. Further, the completed model is used to quantify particular economic-ecologic linkages in the study area. Hopefully, this will lead to a greater understanding of how the economic system and the ecologic system function together in providing both pecuniary and environmental goods.

Chapter 8 discusses the other side of the coin—that is, it discusses the use of a field survey to estimate the demand price of certain environmental goods. More specifically, the analytical framework developed in Chapter 4 for estimating the economic value of environmental goods on the basis of a willingness-to-pay study is given empirical content.

The actual data reported in the ensuing chapters will be identified by source as they are used. In every case, we will make a conscientious effort to describe how the information was obtained and any adjustments that were made for purposes of analysis. These data, however, should be considered as very tentative. They represent the best information currently available, but they are not sacrosanct. We should expect that empirical application of any complicated model of economic-ecologic linkages will require constant attention in order to improve the accuracy of the data and the precision of the results. The work reported here represents an illustration of one approach, but the data are hardly definitive.

NOTE

1. Niles M. Hansen, Rural Poverty and the Urban Crisis (Bloomington: Indiana University Press, 1970), p. 25.

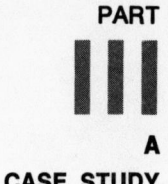

6

As mentioned in earlier chapters, many coastal areas are now considering management plans which allow for residential and industrial activities while providing for the conservation of estuarine and other natural resources. Input-output analysis is a tool which allows one to describe and evaluate the economic impacts of economic growth. It has the additional advantage of being flexible enough to allow for any unusual conditions particular to a given regional resource base.

The discussion of input-output analysis in this chapter is centered on the basic procedures and problems as they apply to the specific study area model. Those desiring a more general discussion of theoretical regional input-output models could see Isard, Chenery, Miernyk, or Leontief.[1] For the more applied aspects of regional input-output analysis one might consult such works as Moore and Peterson, Gamble and Raphael, Tiebout, Moses, Hirsch, or, for a detailed summary, Davis.[2]

THE INPUT-OUTPUT MODEL

As discussed in Chapter 3, the basic model in this study is an application of Leontief input-output analysis. The major advantage of this model is that it can describe the interdependence or relationships between the various sectors and industries in the regional economy. However, the quantity of data needed to describe these interrelationships is enormous, and, therefore, most previous input-output studies have relied primarily on secondary sources of information. Unfortunately, the use of secondary information to build an input-output model has many inherent difficulties. As a result, in this study, emphasis was placed on primary data, with information from secondary sources used to fill in where empirical information was lacking and as a check on the accuracy of the primary data. Though this approach is a costly and time-consuming one, it was felt necessary because two of the implicit objectives of this study were to determine the feasibility of this approach and to develop procedures for facilitating it.

The data for the table were generated for the year 1968. These data were gathered in several ways. Interviews for agriculture and forestry were conducted by the South Carolina Crop Reporting Service. Government, households, institutional, fishing, and professional service establishments were surveyed by one undergraduate and two graduate students working full time during the summer of 1969, with several enumerators being hired for a short period to help with the household survey. The remaining establishments were interviewed by Dun and Bradstreet, Inc., during the fall of 1969.

THE EXPORT BASE ASSUMPTION

The input-output model developed in this study is based on acceptance of the assumptions associated with the export base theory of regional economic growth. The essential element of export base theory is that the impetus for regional growth stems from the sales made by the region to buyers located outside the area.[3] Although export base theory has been thoroughly critiqued[4] and is used with caution by economists, it has found wide acceptance as a planning tool, and the basic notion is to be found implicitly in almost all regional projections.[5]

Following export base theory, in the Charleston area input-output model, all external sales (i.e., sales to buyers outside the area) were aggregated into a single vector which is assumed to constitute the autonomous force in the economy. Internal sales are allocated among each of twenty-eight endogenous sectors. Included in these endogenous sectors are households and governments. These internal sales are considered to be ultimately dependent upon the level and type of external sales. Thus, regional growth is a function of external sales.

DATA COLLECTION AND ORGANIZATION

The use of a field survey as the primary means of generating data for the study necessitated a knowledge of the location and number of business establishments in the study area. Therefore, as the first step in the construction of the Charleston SMSA model, as complete a listing as possible of all establishments in the three-county area was compiled. This "master" list was developed from the South Carolina Industrial Directory, Dun and Bradstreet listings, and Chamber of Commerce information. The list was broken into three sublists by county. The establishments in each county were further divided into twenty-eight sectors, such as agriculture, printing and publishing, real estate, and so on. The aggregation of firms into sectors was based on the Standard Industrial Classification. There were several advantages to using this system, since it allowed utilization of state sales tax data and Dun and Bradstreet sales information, as well as various federal statistics. The industries emphasized (disaggregated) in the study were chosen according to preliminary evidence of their relative economic impact in the study area. From these sector classifications, establishments to be interviewed were randomly selected. With the exception that, where evidence indicated that one or two firms completely dominated a sector, these firms were selected beforehand. The actual size of the sample for each sector was somewhat arbitrary, with the decision being based on two considerations: (1) whether or not the sector was dominated by several large firms and (2) the importance of the sector to the local coastal economy.

The result of this process was that the number of firms chosen for interviews in the individual commercial sectors ranged from 1.3 percent to 83.3 percent. In addition, a 93 percent survey of all government agencies, local, state, and federal, was conducted. A household survey covering 201 households, or .002 percent of the households in the area, was also taken. Sample size relative to each individual sector is shown in Table 2.

The second step in building the input-output table was to obtain a monetary control total for the gross output of each sector. In most cases, state sales tax information was available; in other cases, Dun and Bradstreet sales data were used with survey information to estimate the totals. However, in one case, an indirect estimation procedure had to be followed.

To fill in the body of the table, the survey of commercial establishments, government agencies, and households was used to determine the sales and input structure of the various sectors. However, in a few sectors, information on sales or inputs was very meager, so coefficients from a similar region were assumed to apply to the study area. By similar, it is meant that the region also represents a small local economy, that employment and output and comparable in some sectors, and that in sectors in which coefficients were "borrowed,"

TABLE 2

Employment, Establishments, and Percent Coverage of Sample, by Sector,
Charleston Area Economy, 1968

Sector	Sector Number	SIC Codes	Number of Employees	Number of Establish- ments	Percent of Employment Covered by Sample	Percent of Firms Covered by Sample
Agriculture, Forestry, & Fisheries	1	0913	2,930	290		10.0
Food & Kindred Products	2	2031, 2011-2099	1,600	31	7.5	25.9
Construction & Mining	3	1441, 1511-1599, 1711-1799	5,612	399		
Textile & Apparel Mfg.	4	2211-2299, 2311-2399	3,364	18	10.4	49.9
Lumber, Pulp, & Paper Prods.	5	2411-2499, 2611-2661	4,336	41	44.6	36.8
Furniture & Fixtures Mfg.	6	2511-2599	239	7	66.9	71.4
Printers & Publishers	7	2711-2799	823	24	54.0	25.0
Chemical Manufacturing	8	2812-2899	1,277	17	24.6	41.2
Petroleum & Coal Mfg.	9	2911-2999	434	6	16.6	83.3
Rubber, Plastic, & Related Mfg.	10	3011-3099	1,040	4	1.2	25.0
Stone, Clay, & Glass Prods. Mfg.	11	3211-3299	1,351	21	62.5	23.8
Machinery, Repairs, and Metal Shops	12	3312-3399, 3731-3732, 3411-3499, 3511-3599 (Exp. 3531-3532)	3,644	44	90.5	58.8
Miscellaneous Manufacturing	13	1911-1999, 3111-3199 2111-2141, 3911-3999 3811-3872	2,174	10		
Transportation	14	4111-4721	3,411	55	2.5	25.4
Communications	15	4811-4833	1,035	19	6.0	31.6
Utilities	16	4911-4931	1,300	6	42.9	83.3
Eating & Drinking Places	17	5811-5891	2,342	250	4.5	8.0
Hotels & Lodging Places	18	7011	3,000	78	5.1	10.3
Gasoline Service Stations	19	5541	883	221	1.0	7.2
Other Wholesale & Retail Trade	20	5011-5999 (Exp 5811- 5899, 5541)	14,525	2,533	6.0	1.3
Finance & Insurance	21	6011-6499	2,853	232	7.0	3.0
Real Estate	22	6511-6699	774	122	4.8	8.2
Other Business & Professional	23	7211-8999	13,949	6,858	1.9	7.8
Local & State Government				24		79.2
Defense-Related Government				5*		100.0
Other Federal Government				30		100.0
Households			5,600	87,369	1.7	0.2
Other Establishments			1,000	43	10.1	13.9

*Most of the purchasing of the thirteen separate naval installations is through the Charleston Naval Supply Depot.

Source: U.S. Bureau of the Census, County Business Patterns, 1968, South Carolina; Dun and Bradstreet unpublished data; Charleston Area Survey, 1968.

the employment and output figures were especially comparable between the two economies. It was felt that these "borrowed" coefficients would be more appropriate than applying national coefficients directly to the Charleston area. The portion of gross output, used locally, multiplied by these regional input and sales coefficients completed each sector where survey information was felt to be lacking.* Modifications in the sales and input structure of these sectors were made until the table appeared reasonable in light of all available information.

DATA ESTIMATION PROCEDURES

The estimation procedure for gross output varied for the different sectors of the region's economy. In most sectors, total output figures were available in detail from state sales tax data, while for others reasonable estimates were developed from Dun and Bradstreet sales data and from survey information. The estimation procedure employed for the finance and insurance sector differed considerably and is discussed below.

Gross output for the finance and insurance sector was not available, so an indirect estimation procedure following the method used by Canion and Trock was employed.[6] Bank deposits in the area were used as the control or output total for finance. This total was added to the available figures for gross output of the insurance sector and the resulting sum was multiplied by a value-added coefficient (value-added as a percent of sales) to eliminate double counting. This procedure provided a figure that appeared very reasonable in light of other available information.

Sales and input data generated by the field survey were considerably more disaggregated than the sectors appearing in the matrix. To fill in the body of the endogenous matrix, it was necessary to aggregate the data in several cases to avoid disclosure problems. The endogenous part of the matrix was developed from two separate matrixes. Survey and secondary information was utilized to build independently an internal matrix from both input and sales data. The final endogenous matrix is the result of combining these two tables.

---

*In this vein, it was interesting to note that firms interviewed seemed to have little apparent preference as to whether they supplied information on input or sales distributions.

Ideally, every sale by a sector should have a corresponding purchase by another sector, and a matrix built from input information should correspond to one built from sales information. However, this was not always the case. During the process of balancing the two matrixes, when a choice existed between a sales and an input figure, the one chosen depended on the overall questionnaire responses to the distribution of both sales and inputs for the particular sector. Consequently, this caused some unfortunate, but necessary, arbitrariness in the distribution of money flows among the sectors.

The most crucial data problem for a regional input-output model is often that concerned with imports and exports or external money flows. There exists no appropriate secondary check for the external flows.[7] Due to this, external sales were estimated by paying especially close attention in the field survey to the division of a firm's output into the appropriate category—internal or external. In addition, the summing of individual sector row and column values and the subtracting of this total from the gross control totals provided a useful check; however, survey information was assumed to be accurate unless there was an unreconcilable deviation from internal flow data.

After the data were compiled into the matrix, various checks were made against secondary sources. For example, a comparison of total personal income with a comparable figure showed a discrepancy of only $81,810, or .001 percent.[8] However, we were not always so fortunate. The field survey estimate for the total cost of materials for manufacturing industries differed from the 1967 Census of Manufacturing estimate by .28 percent.[9] All things considered, the field survey appeared to provide reasonably accurate data, except, of course, in the sectors where survey information was weak and additional estimation procedures had to be employed.

THE TRANSACTIONS TABLE

The transactions table or flows table includes all of the goods and services produced in the local economy. The transactions table for the Charleston area study is summarized in Table 3. The method of reading the table is simple. Each sector appears twice in the system, as a producer of outputs and as a user of inputs. The entries in each row of the table represent the amount of a sector output that is consumed by itself, by each of the other sectors in the local economy, and by final demand. For example, reading across the first row, the agriculture, forestry, and fishery sector sold $2,422,913 worth of output to itself. It sold $3,539,593 of output to the food and

TABLE 3

Interindustry Transactions, Charleston Study Area Input-Output Model, 1968

	Agriculture, Forestry, & Fisheries (1)	Food & Kindred Products (2)	Construction & Mining (3)	Textile & Apparel (4)	Lumber, Pulp & Paper Products (5)	Furniture & Fixtures Mfg. (6)	Printers & Publishers (7)
1. Agriculture, Forestry, & Fisheries	$2,422,913	3,539,593	0	0	4,800,047	0	0
2. Food & Kindred Products	0	2,101,023	0	0	0	0	0
3. Construction & Mining	8,016	0	59,368,542	0	1,418,992	235	0
4. Textile & Apparel Mfg.	0	37,296	0	22,938	8,759	0	0
5. Lumber, Pulp, & Paper Prods.	0	3,552	2,644,452	0	1,856,952	1,178,853	1,090,034
6. Furniture & Fixture Mfg.	0	0	0	205	8,759	235	0
7. Printers & Publishers	0	33,744	11,448	0	0	1,882	119,719
8. Chemical Manufacturing	0	62,160	572,392	0	1,357,678	0	0
9. Petroleum & Coal Mfg.	0	8,880	0	819	796	1,176	10,046
10. Rubber, Plastic, & Related Mfg.	0	39,072	560,944	0	148,906	0	0
11. Stone, Clay, & Glass Products	6,012	0	366,331	0	0	0	0
12. Machinery, Repairs, & Metal Shops	184,373	0	0	819	0	2,588	22,604
13. Miscellaneous Manufacturing	0	8,880	251,853	5,939	35,037	0	837
14. Transportation	46,093	0	286,196	3,072	182,916	235	34,325
15. Communications	0	15,984	34,343	0	0	0	3,348
16. Utilities	52,106	170,497	11,448	0	254,017	170,122	0
17. Eating & Drinking Places	0	0	0	2,048	8,759	0	0
18. Hotels & Lodging Places	0	0	0	0	8,759	0	0
19. Gasoline Service Stations	366,743	35,520	12,237,750	0	0	0	0
20. Other Wholesale & Retail Trade	6,557,298	94,128	629,632	205	2,058,414	21,883	187,533
21. Finance & Insurance	432,878	0	343,435	614	52,555	0	0
22. Real Estate	0	0	0	390,976	0	941	930,129
23. Other Business & Professional Services	1,270,577	371,187	2,243,778	15,155	218,980	235	107,999
24. Local & State Government	8,016	99,457	57,239	0	43,796	0	0
25. Defense-Related Government	0	0	0	0	0	0	0
26. Other Federal Government	0	0	0	1,262,226	0	0	0
27. Households	7,962,146	6,416,734	23,582,568	1,262,226	17,938,862	867,080	4,561,902
28. Unallocated	0	0	0	0	0	0	0
29. Total Local	19,317,171	13,037,707	103,202,351	1,705,016	30,402,984	2,245,465	7,068,476
30. Total External	723,470	4,722,420	11,276,133	343,054	57,189,116	107,535	1,303,523
31. Total	$20,040,641	17,760,127	114,478,484	2,048,070	87,592,100	2,353,000	8,371,999

(continued)

(Table 3, continued)

	Chemical Manufacturing (8)	Petroleum & Coal Mfg. (9)	Rubber, Plastic, & Related Mfg. (10)	Stone, Clay, & Glass Prods. Mfg. (11)	Machinery, Repairs, & Metal Shops (12)	Miscellaneous Manufacturing (13)	Transportation (14)	Communications (15)
1.	$0	0	0	0	0	0	0	0
2.	716	272	692	1,069	0	3,973	0	0
3.	0	0	0	312,919	4,599,005	0	631,943	14,057
4.	5,014	68	0	0	8,008	3,841	0	0
5.	24,354	2,716	0	0	0	9,403	0	0
6.	0	339	0	0	0	1,059	0	0
7.	716	0	9,347	47,758	5,338	2,384	2,290	9,957
8.	536,501	33,266	743,984	79,121	10,677	2,516	0	0
9.	0	0	0	0	37,368	0	0	0
10.	15,042	204	93,128	12,830	13,346	30,197	0	0
11.	0	0	0	0	0	0	0	0
12.	0	0	0	0	715,341	0	0	0
13.	4,298	0	17,656	6,059	149,474	86,088	0	0
14.	105,294	0	0	0	0	0	0	0
15.	33,665	16,972	16,964	1,069	298,949	397	858,619	23,135
16.	0	0	0	0	870,154	20,264	66,400	24,014
17.	2,865	0	0	0	0	0	41,214	0
18.	0	0	0	0	0	0	0	0
19.	7,879	0	0	0	2,669	0	151,117	5,857
20.	0	50,895	0	0	298,949	0	1,524,907	60,035
21.	26,503	2,987	17,310	0	53,384	9,006	36,634	0
22.	20,056	0	0	0	0	0	29,765	11,128
23.	1,003,521	5,770	76,510	60,232	24,023	15,893	38,924	0
24.	8,595	407	346	1,426	29,361	795	6,869	14,056
25.	0	0	0	0	0	0	0	0
26.	0	0	0	0	0	0	0	0
27.	2,008,475	389,553	1,688,071	2,802,015	13,676,902	517,454	17,634,884	1,323,983
28.	0	0	0	0	0	0	0	229,010
29.	3,803,494	503,539	2,664,008	3,324,498	20,792,948	703,270	21,023,566	1,715,232
30.	3,359,400	175,361	797,992	239,509	5,898,899	621,157	1,872,934	1,213,286
31.	7,162,894	678,900	3,462,000	3,562,000	26,691,847	1,324,427	22,896,500	2,928,518

	Utilities (16)	Eating & Drinking Places (17)	Hotels & Lodging Places (18)	Gasoline Service Stations (19)	Other Wholesale & Retail Trade (20)	Finance & Insurance (21)	Real Estate (22)	Other Bus. & Professional Services (23)
1.	$ 0	0	0	0	157,962	0	0	4,842,296
2.	0	3,499,861	464,527	0	726,625	0	0	116,215
3.	1,231,698	98,926	112,959	165,135	52,654	135,996	18,242,604	796,904
4.	0	0	1,269	66,054	368,577	36,756	9,322	271,169
5.		0	2,538	0	421,232	29,404	11,652	0
6.	5,637	0	2,538	0	947,772	0	18,643	2,556,732
7.	2,818	0	6,346	0	1,000,426	452,094	27,965	326,902
8.	11,274	0	20,307	0	526,539	0	0	0
9.	0	0	11,423	148,621	52,654	62,484	13,983	520,201
10.	0	0	0	0	1,000,426	0	0	0
11.	0	0	1,269	0	0	11,037	0	0
12.	1,321,890	0	0	20,642	0	75,729	6,991	0
13.	14,093		0	33,027	8,108,715	0	0	138,351
14.	5,637	2,674	2,538	28,898	157,962	319,774	34,956	88,545
15.	16,911	10,695	20,307	0	3,422,510	0	0	1,023,800
16.	118,378	1,326,150	340,146	0	0	0	0	1,361,377
17.	2,818	0	0	0	0	0	0	0
18.	0	251,327	20,307	61,926	0	0	0	0
19.	5,637	0	0	24,245,898	21,904,062	1,043,860	340,243	13,973,482
20.	5,211,462	6,948,922	4,169,322	70,182	6,529,095	7,395,235	659,512	913,119
21.	22,548	0	72,344	0	315,924	2,359,712	405,495	2,452,653
22.	0	0	0	206,418	10,899,377	1,275,421	1,582,362	4,543,457
23.	186,023	40,105	2,538	268,344	8,003,407	0	67,582	370,781
24.	419,961	751,307	187,842	0	0	0	0	0
25.	0	0	0	0	0	0	0	0
26.	0	0	0	0	0	0	0	0
27.	8,915,010	4,711,043	5,430,907	7,984,261				10,514,699
28.	0	0	0	4,128	56,866,314	13,610,615	817,981	7,797,480
29.	17,491,795	17,641,010	10,869,427	33,303,534	121,462,233	26,808,107	22,239,291	52,618,163
30.	10,693,503	9,095,895	1,822,573	7,980,133	405,077,709	9,947,536	1,065,007	2,722,359
31.	$28,185,298	26,736,905	12,692,000	41,283,667	526,539,942	36,755,643	23,304,298	55,340,522

(continued)

(TABLE 3, continued)

	Local & State Government (24)	Defense-Related Government (25)	Other Federal Government (26)	Households (27)	Unallocated (28)	Total Local (29)	Total External (30)	Total (31)
1.	$0	0	0	937,300	0	16,700,111	3,340,530	20,040,641
2.	58,670	34,772	5,074	4,181,800	0	11,195,289	6,564,838	17,760,127
3.	2,352,157	5,007,136	2,171,508	5,047,000	25,356	101,793,507	12,684,977	114,478,884
4.	10,667	0	0	0	2,415	852,388	1,195,682	2,048,070
5.	10,667	0	5,074	3,749,200	4,830	9,954,879	77,637,221	87,592,100
6.	21,335	0	0	72,100	10,867	1,070,611	1,282,389	2,353,000
7.	58,670	0	169,966	2,884,000	0	8,362,946	9,053	8,371,999
8.	64,004	104,315	27,905	0	1,207	4,630,314	2,532,580	7,162,894
9.	149,343	34,772	17,758	0	9,660	471,275	207,625	678,900
10.	0	0	0	0	1,207	2,524,011	937,989	3,462,000
11.	24,335	0	2,537	2,018,800	1,207	2,420,491	1,143,507	3,563,998
12.	74,672	0	78,641	3,677,100	0	6,083,686	20,608,161	26,691,847
13.	5,334	0	58,273	576,800	0	1,317,576	6,851	1,324,427
14.	128,008	0	10,147	72,100	4,830	9,991,921	12,904,579	22,896,500
15.	64,004	0	45,663	1,586,200	0	2,919,425	9,093	2,928,518
16.	256,017	869,294	284,122	6,200,600	3,622	15,461,823	12,723,475	28,185,298
17.	10,667	0	2,537	6,921,600	19,319	8,329,942	18,406,963	26,736,905
18.	10,667	0	22,831	144,200	0	460,139	12,231,861	12,692,000
19.	138,676	0	7,610	16,294,600	1,207	17,079,441	24,204,226	41,283,667
20.	1,301,420	7,927,966	20,294	320,556,600	0	430,431,869	96,108,073	526,539,942
21.	133,342	0	1,220,205	18,169,200	2,415	36,751,835	3,808	36,755,643
22.	405,360	0	2,537	14,852,600	2,069,554	23,278,833	25,465	23,304,298
23.	1,109,407	0	187,724	28,551,600	18,112	55,253,985	86,537	55,340,522
24.	922,728	0	22,831	0	8,452	11,416,987	41,919,901	53,336,888
25.	0	0	0	0	0	0	347,717,801	347,717,801
26.	0	0	0	0	0	0	25,368,088	25,368,088
27.	43,970,930	300,010,919	18,386,790	126,030,800	0	699,883,124	21,116,876	721,000,000
28.	1,573,438	0	116,693	3,316,600	789,667	13,827,016	1,221,325	15,048,341
29.	52,854,518	313,989,174	22,861,720	565,840,800	2,973,927	1,492,463,424		
30.	482,370	33,728,627	2,506,368	155,159,200	12,074,414		742,199,474	
31.	$53,336,888	$347,717,801	25,368,088	721,000,000	15,048,341			2,234,662,898

Source: Charleston Area Survey, 1969; South Carolina State Sales Tax Records; Dun and Brodstreet Sales Data.

kindred products sector, and so on. The final entry in the row represents the total dollar output of the sector—$20,040,641 for sector one.

Sector one, however, is also a purchaser of inputs. Each column of Table 3 represents the sector's input structure. Reading down column one, it can be seen that sector one bought $2,422,913 of products from itself. It purchased no inputs from food and kindred products, but purchased $8,016 worth of products from construction and mining. The last figure in the column represents total outlays. The input structure of all other sectors can be determined in the same way.

TECHNICAL COEFFICIENTS

The table of technical coefficients shows the direct purchases of a given industry from all other industries for each dollar of output. A specific technical coefficient then represents the amount of goods and services required from one local industry to produce a unit of output of another local industry. Table 4 illustrates the matrix of technical coefficients for the Charleston study area.*

The table of technical coefficients matrix is read in the same way as Table 3. Reading down the first column, we can see that each dollar of output by sector 1 requires direct purchases from itself of 12.09 cents, .0004 cents from sector 3, 32.72 cents from sector 20, and so on. The total direct purchases figure, .9368, indicates how much sector 1 must buy from all sectors in order for it to produce one dollar of output.

INTERDEPENDENCE COEFFICIENTS

Table 5 represents the matrix of direct and indirect coefficients. As mentioned, Table 3 shows the direct purchases needed by a particular sector to produce one dollar of output. However, this does not represent the total additional output resulting from an increase in sales

---

*The technical coefficients are calculated directly from the data in Table 3. To compute the coefficients, each entry in a given sector column is divided by the column total.

TABLE 4

Technical Coefficients Matrix, Charleston Study Area
Input-Output Model, 1968

	Agriculture, Forestry, & Fisheries (1)	Food & Kindred Products (2)	Construction & Mining (3)	Textile & Apparel (4)	Lumber, Pulp, & Paper Prods. (5)	Furniture & Fixtures Mfg. (6)	Printers & Publishers (7)
1. Agriculture, Forestry, & Fisheries	$ .1209	.1993	0	.0000	.0548	0	0
2. Food & Kindred Products	0	.1183	0	0	0	0	0
3. Construction & Mining	.0004	0	.5186	0	.0162	0	0
4. Textile & Apparel Mfg.	0	.0021	0	.0112	.0001	.0001	0
5. Lumber, Pulp, & Paper Prods.	0	.0002	.0231	0	.0212	.5010	0
6. Furniture & Fixture Mfg.	0	0	0	.0001	.0001	0	0
7. Printers & Publishers	0	.0019	.0001	0	0	.0001	.1302
8. Chemical Manufacturing	0	.0035	.0050	0	.0155	.0008	.0143
9. Petroleum & Coal Mfg.	0	.0005	0	0	.0005	0	0
10. Rubber, Plastic, & Related Mfg.	0	.0022	.0049	.0004	.0017	.0005	.0012
11. Stone, Clay, & Glass Prods. Mfg.	.0003	0	.0032	0	0	0	0
12. Machinery, Repairs, & Metal Shops	.0092	0	0	0	0	0	0
13. Miscellaneous Manufacturing	0	.0005	.0022	.0004	.0004	.0011	.0027
14. Transportation	.0023	0	.0025	.0029	.0208	0	.0001
15. Communications	0	.0009	.0003	.0015	0	.0001	.0041
16. Utilities	.0026	.0096	.0001	0	.0029	.0723	.0004
17. Eating & Drinking Places	0	0	0	0	.0001	0	0
18. Hotels & Lodging Places	0	0	0	.0010	.0001	0	0
19. Gasoline Service Stations	.0183	.0020	0	0	0	0	0
20. Other Wholesale & Retail Trade	.3272	0	.1069	0	.0235	0	0
21. Finance & Insurance	.0216	.0053	.0055	.0001	.0006	.0093	.0224
22. Real Estate	0	0	.0030	.0003	0	0	0
23. Other Business & Professional Services	.0634	.0209	.0196	.1909	.0025	.0004	.1111
24. Local & State Government	.0004	.0056	.0005	.0074	.0005	.0001	.0129
25. Defense-Related Government	0	0	0	0	0	0	0
26. Other Federal Government	0	0	0	0	0	0	0
27. Households	.3973	.3613	.2060	.6163	.2048	.3685	.5449
28. Unallocated	0.	0	0	0	0	0	0
29. Total Local	$ .9368	.7341	.9017	.8327	.3664	.9543	.8443

	Chemical Manufacturing (8)	Petroleum & Coal Mfg. (9)	Rubber, Plastic, & Related Mfg. (10)	Stone, Clay, & Glass Prods. Mfg. (11)	Machinery, Repairs, & Metal Shops (12)	Miscellaneous Manufacturing (13)	Transportation (14)	Communications (15)
1.	$ 0	0	0	0	0	0	0	0
2.	.0001	.0004	.0002	.0003	0	.0030	0	0
3.	0	0	0	.0878	.1723	0	.0276	.0048
4.	.0007	.0001	0	0	.0003	.0029	0	0
5.	.0034	.0040	0	0	0	.0071	0	0
6.	0	.0005	0	0	0	.0008	0	0
7.	.0001	0	.0027	.0134	.0002	.0018	.0001	.0034
8.	.0749	.0490	.2149	.0222	.0004	.0019	0	0
9.	0	0	0	0	.0014	0	0	0
10.	.0021	.0003	.0269	.0036	.0005	.0228	0	0
11.	0	0	0	0	0	0	0	0
12.	0	0	0	0	.0268	0	0	0
13.	.0006	0	.0051	.0017	.0056	.0650	.0375	.0079
14.	.0147	0	0	0	0	0	.0029	.0082
15.	.0047	.0250	.0049	.0003	.0112	.0003	.0018	0
16.	0	0	0	0	.0326	.0153	0	0
17.	.0004	0	0	0	0	0	0	0
18.	0	0	0	0	0	0	.0066	.0020
19.	.0011	0	0	0	.0001	0	.0666	.0205
20.	0	.0751	0	0	.0112	0	.0016	0
21.	.0037	.0044	.0050	0	.0020	.0068	.0013	.0038
22.	.0028	0	0	0	0	0	.0017	0
23.	.1401	.0085	.0221	.0169	.0009	.0120	.0003	.0048
24.	.0012	.0006	.0001	.0004	.0011	.0006	0	0
25.	0	0	0	0	0	0	0	0
26.	0	0	0	0	0	0	0	0
27.	.2804	.5738	.4876	.7862	.5124	.3907	.7702	.4521
28.	0	0	0	0	0	0	0	.0782
29.	$ .5313	.7419	.7696	.9329	.7791	.5311	.9182	.5856

(continued)

(TABLE 4, continued)

	Utilities (16)	Eating & Drinking Places (17)	Hotels & Lodging Places (18)	Gasoline Service Stations (19)	Other Wholesale & Retail Trade (20)	Finance & Insurance (21)	Real Estate (22)	Other Bus. & Professional Services (23)
1.	$0	0	0	0	.0003	0	0	.0875
2.		.1309	.0366	0	.0138	0	0	.0021
3.	.0437	.0037	.0089	.0040	.0001	.0037	.7828	.0144
4.	0	0	.0001	.0016	.0007	.0010	.0004	.0049
5.	0	0	.0002	0	.0008	.0008	.0005	0
6.	.0002	0	.0002	0	.0018	0	0	0
7.	.0001	0	.0005	0	.0019	.0123	.0008	.0462
8.	.0004	0	.0016	.0036	.0010	0	.0012	.0059
9.	0	0	.0009	0	.0001	.0017	0	0
10.	0	0	0	0	.0019	0	.0006	.0094
11.	0	0	.0001	.0005	0	.0003	0	0
12.	.0469	0	0	0	0	.0007	0	0
13.	.0005	0	0	0	0	0	.0003	0
14.	.0002	.0001	.0002	.0008	.0154	0	0	.0025
15.	.0006	.0004	.0016	.0007	.0003	.0087	.0015	.0016
16.	.0042	.0496	.0268	0	.0065	0	0	.0185
17.	.0001	0	0	0	0	0	0	.0246
18.	0	.0094	.0016	.0015	0	0	0	0
19.	.0002	0	0	.5873	0	0	0	0
20.	.1849	.2599	.3285	.0017	.0416	.0284	.0146	.2525
21.	.0008	0	.0057	0	.0124	.2012	.0283	.0165
22.	0	0	0	.0050	.0006	.0642	.0174	.0445
23.	.0066	.0015	.0002	.0065	.0207	.0347	.0679	.0821
24.	.0149	.0281	.0148	0	.0152	0	.0029	.0067
25.	0	0	0	0	0	0	0	0
26.	0	0	0	0	0	0	0	0
27.	.3163	.1762	.4279	.1934	.1080	.3703	.0351	.1900
28.	0			.0001	0	0	0	.1409
29.	$.6207	.6597	.8564	.8067	.2429	.7280	.9544	.9508

74

	Local & State Government (24)	Defense-Related Government (25)	Other Federal Government (26)	Households (27)	Unallocated (28)
1.	$ 0	0	0	.0013	0
2.	.0011	.0001	.0002	.0058	0
3.	.0441	.0144	.0856	.0070	.0021
4.	.0002	0	0	0	.0002
5.	.0002	0	.0002	.0052	.0004
6.	.0004	0	0	.0001	.0009
7.	.0011	0	.0067	.0040	0
8.	.0012	.0003	.0011	0	.0001
9.	.0028	.0001	.0007	0	.0008
10.	0	0	0	0	.0001
11.	.0004	0	.0001	.0028	.0001
12.	.0014	0	.0031	.0051	0
13.	.0001	0	.0021	.0008	0
14.	.0024	0	.0004	.0001	.0004
15.	.0012	0	.0018	.0022	0
16.	.0048	.0025	.0112	.0086	.0003
17.	.0002	0	.0001	.0096	.0016
18.	.0002	0	.0009	.0002	0
19.	.0026	0	.0003	.0226	.0001
20.	.0244	.0228	.0008	.4445	0
21.	.0025	0	.0481	.0252	.0002
22.	.0076	0	.0001	.0206	.1714
23	.0208	0	.0074	.0396	.0015
24.	.0173	0	.0009	0	.0007
25.	0	0	0	0	0
26.	0	0	0	0	0
27.	.8244	.8628	.7248	.1748	0
28.	.0295	0	.0046	.0022	.0654
29.	$ .9912	.9355	.9010	.6246	.2459

Source: Calculated from data in Table 3.

TABLE 5

Elements of the Leontief Inverse, Charleston Study Area
Input-Output Model, 1968

	Agriculture, Forestry, & Fisheries (1)	Food & Kindred Products (2)	Construction & Mining (3)	Textile & Apparel (4)	Lumber & Wood Products (5)	Furniture & Fixtures Mfg. (6)	Printers & Publishers (7)
1. Agriculture, Forestry, & Fisheries	$1.1573	.2712	.0177	.0331	.0694	.0411	.0260
2. Food & Kindred Products	.0190	1.1476	.0150	.0169	.0067	.0117	.0161
3. Construction & Mining	.0765	.0627	2.1490	.0977	.0638	.0766	.0912
4. Textiles & Apparel Mfg.	.0015	.0034	.0012	1.0133	.0005	.0008	.0016
5. Lumber, Pulp, & Paper Prods.	.0070	.0063	.0554	.0081	1.0255	.5180	.0079
6. Furniture & Fixtures Mfg.	.0015	.0009	.0012	.0012	.0005	1.0008	.0010
7. Printers & Publishers	.0135	.0125	.0107	.0207	.0043	.0074	1.1670
8. Chemical Manufacturing	.0035	.0074	.0175	.0047	.0189	.0118	.0220
9. Petroleum & Coal Mfg.	.0003	.0008	.0002	.0002	.0006	.0004	.0002
10. Rubber, Plastic, & Related Mfg.	.0035	.0050	.0133	.0048	.0030	.0032	.0052
11. Stone, Clay, & Glass Prods. Mfg.	.0026	.0022	.0087	.0028	.0012	.0021	.0028
12. Machinery, Repairs, & Metal Shops	.0156	.0074	.0042	.0058	.0029	.0079	.0057
13. Miscellaneous Manufacturing	.0011	.0015	.0059	.0017	.0010	.0023	.0046
14. Transportation	.0165	.0090	.0168	.0129	.0267	.0181	.0097
15. Communications	.0031	.0036	.0032	.0048	.0014	.0026	.0083
16. Utilities	.0183	.0234	.0126	.0175	.0088	.0843	.0165
17. Eating & Drinking Places	.0102	.0090	.0086	.0152	.0043	.0077	.0135
18. Hotels & Lodging Places	.0002	.0002	.0002	.0013	.0002	.0002	.0003
19. Gasoline Service Stations	.0372	.0230	.0150	.0204	.0093	.0159	.0204
20. Other Wholesale & Retail Trade	.7980	.4693	.5879	.5214	.2351	.3864	.5008
21. Finance & Insurance	.0709	.0479	.0487	.0454	.0190	.0430	.0754
22. Real Estate	.0305	.0255	.0311	.0424	.0116	.0213	.0394
23. Other Business & Professional Services	.1385	.0846	.0981	.2739	.0347	.0511	.2049
24. Local & State Government	.0150	.0156	.0119	.0191	.0050	.0086	.0256
25. Defense-Related Government	0	0	0	0	0	0	0
26. Other Federal Government	0	0	0	0	0	0	0
27. Households	.6991	.6911	.6412	.8687	.3420	.6604	.8707
28. Unallocated	.0232	.0167	.0169	.0443	.0063	.0097	.0344
29. Total Local	3.1636	2.9478	3.7922	3.0983	1.9027	2.9934	3.1712

	Chemical Manufacturing (8)	Petroleum & Coal Mfg. (9)	Rubber, Plastic, & Related Mfg. (10)	Stone, Clay, & Glass Prods. Mfg. (11)	Machinery, Repairs, & Metal Shops (12)	Miscellaneous Manufacturing (13)	Transportation (14)	Communications (15)
1.	$ .0238	.0121	.0157	.0163	.0117	.0100	.0134	.0077
2.	.0101	.0145	.0131	.0182	.0141	.0131	.0180	.0101
3.	.0682	.0597	.0648	.2627	.4332	.0456	.1359	.0846
4.	.0021	.0010	.0012	.0011	.0012	.0038	.0010	.0006
5.	.0086	.0108	.0071	.0129	.0154	.0128	.0097	.0058
6.	.0070	.0014	.0008	.0011	.0009	.0014	.0012	.0007
7.	.0144	.0090	.0142	.0275	.0090	.0090	.0107	.0101
8.	1.0848	.0553	.2414	.0293	.0055	.0098	.0030	.0019
9.	.0001	1.0001	.0001	.0002	.0016	.0001	.0002	.0002
10.	.0054	.0025	1.0307	.0074	.0046	.0265	.0028	.0016
11.	.0016	.0023	.0023	1.0038	.0036	.0017	.0033	.0019
12.	.0033	.0047	.0046	.0038	1.0340	.0042	.0063	.0040
13.	.0014	.0010	.0067	.0064	.0081	1.0704	.0014	.0008
14.	.0225	.0092	.0109	.0036	.0094	.0056	1.0496	.0059
15.	.0073	.0280	.0088	.0039	.0144	.0024	.0063	1.0099
16.	.0109	.0121	.0121	.0158	.0459	.0250	.0170	.0170
17.	.0101	.0090	.0010	.0125	.0091	.0067	.0115	.0068
18.	.0002	.0002	.0002	.0003	.0003	.0002	.0003	.0002
19.	.0126	.0175	.0173	.0240	.0181	.0128	.0299	.0155
20.	.3064	.4768	.4008	.5672	.4698	.2960	.6052	.3312
21.	.0319	.0406	.0418	.0483	.0407	.0342	.0477	.0269
22.	.0306	.0250	.0278	.0338	.0259	.0184	.0321	.0364
23.	.2027	.0688	.1113	.0966	.0625	.0537	.0702	.0413
24.	.0085	.0096	.0084	.0114	.0106	.0066	.0114	.0113
25.	0	0	0	0	0	0	0	0
26.	0	0	0	0	0	0	0	0
27.	.4767	.7558	.7335	1.0397	.7828	.5533	1.0060	.5817
28.	.0325	.0148	.0195	.0177	.0128	.0098	.0138	.0924
29.	2.3837	2.6418	2.7961	3.3726	3.0452	2.2331	3.1079	2.3065

(continued)

(Table 5, continued)

	Utilities (16)	Eating & Drinking Places (17)	Hotels & Lodging Places (18)	Gasoline Service Stations (19)	Other Wholesale & Retail Trade (20)	Finance & Insurance (21)	Real Estate (22)
1.	$ .0089	.0419	.0203	.0094	.0096	.0152	.0239
2.	.0119	.1608	.0582	.0161	.0202	.0126	.0150
3.	.1515	.0522	.0754	.0442	.0262	.2026	1.7372
4.	.0007	.0010	.0012	.0026	.0012	.0023	.0019
5.	.0073	.0045	.0068	.0045	.0038	.0102	.0461
6.	.0011	.0010	.0015	.0015	.0021	.0008	.0012
7.	.0067	.0063	.0089	.0065	.0062	.0281	.0155
8.	.0030	.0026	.0045	.0025	.0026	.0043	.0167
9.	.0002	.0003	.0012	.0038	.0002	.0001	.0002
10.	.0023	.0022	.0026	.0024	.0029	.0053	.0125
11.	.0019	.0014	.0022	.0012	.0007	.0025	.0073
12.	.0517	.0056	.0056	.0031	.0017	.0046	.0042
13.	.0018	.0007	.0009	.0007	.0004	.0022	.0052
14.	.0088	.0091	.0121	.0145	.0190	.0080	.0154
15.	.0030	.0023	.0042	.0024	.0013	.0136	.0050
16.	1.0151	.0603	.0397	.0102	.0109	.0115	.0136
17.	.0062	1.0052	.0077	.0048	.0030	.0091	.0101
18.	.0002	.0095	1.0018	.0001	.0001	.0002	.0002
19.	.0120	.0108	.0154	1.0103	.0051	.0155	.0147
20.	.4767	.5247	.6990	.8202	1.1665	.4198	.5689
21.	.0280	.0260	.0425	.0293	.0268	1.2883	.0827
22.	.0174	.0150	.0218	.0143	.0103	.1073	1.0542
23.	.0487	.0444	.0549	.0468	.0409	.1058	.1660
24.	.0238	.0394	.0278	.0202	.0188	.0088	.0150
25.	0	0	0	0	0	0	0
26.	0	0	0	0	0	0	0
27.	.5085	.4224	.6536	.3758	.2094	.6659	.6199
28.	.0095	.0091	.0110	.0088	.0074	.0189	.0274
29.	2.4069	1.5540	2.7808	2.4865	1.5973	2.9635	4.4798

	Other Bus. & Professional Services (23)	Local & State Government (24)	Defense-Related Government (25)	Other Federal Government (26)	Households (27)	Unallocated (28)
1.	.1224	.0170	.0139	.0144	.0148	.0048
2.	.0217	.0202	.0185	.0171	.0199	.0032
3.	.2164	.1997	.1756	.2633	.0855	.3245
4.	.0066	.0014	.0010	.0011	.0011	.0006
5.	.0094	.0122	.0110	.0128	.0096	.0095
6.	.0014	.0017	.0012	.0011	.0012	.0012
7.	.0669	.0139	.0110	.0195	.0119	.0030
8.	.0141	.0054	.0036	.0054	.0028	.0033
9.	.0003	.0031	.0003	.0009	.0002	.0009
10.	.0140	.0034	.0030	.0036	.0026	.0025
11.	.0023	.0041	.0036	.0037	.0037	.0015
12.	.0056	.0083	.0067	.0098	.0073	.0008
13.	.0014	.0018	.0015	.0040	.0014	.0010
14.	.0149	.0137	.0106	.0105	.0108	.0034
15.	.0047	.0050	.0035	.0057	.0038	.0010
16.	.0333	.0215	.0182	.0262	.0172	.0031
17.	.0341	.0131	.0122	.0116	.0136	.0037
18.	.0004	.0006	.0003	.0016	.0003	.0001
19.	.0147	.0275	.0247	.0229	.0277	.0029
20.	.6523	.6100	.5917	.5410	.6214	.1098
21.	.0619	.0531	.0480	.1057	.0522	.0158
22.	.1004	.0484	.0324	.0361	.0356	.1938
23.	1.1693	.0987	.0721	.0808	.0769	.0330
24.	.0213	1.0292	.0109	.0114	.0114	.0036
25.	0	0	1.0000	0	0	0
26.	0	0	0	1.0000	0	0
27.	.5381	1.0803	1.0764	.9849	1.2054	.1201
28.	.1778	.0503	.0140	.0202	.0151	1.0754
29.	3.3003	3.3436	3.1659	3.2153	2.2534	1.9225

Source: Calculated from data in Table 4.

to final demand, only the direct effect.* There are also indirect
effects of the increased exports. For instance, if sector 1 increases
export production, it must purchase additional inputs from all its
supplying sectors. They, in turn, must increase production and purchase more from their supplying sectors. Table 5 isolates these
direct and indirect effects. Each coefficient in the table shows the
direct and indirect requirements of a column for a row output per
$1 of output delivered to final demand.

The data in Table 5 are sometimes called the Leontief inverse.
It is the matrix designated in Chapter 3 as A'. In essence, these data
are the empirical heart of the model, the vital input which will be
molded in the following chapter with an environmental matrix to
estimate the total direct and indirect environmental impact of specific
changes in the level of local economic activity.

BRIEF DESCRIPTIVE ANALYSIS OF THE
CHARLESTON ECONOMY

Examination of Table 3 (rows and columns 31 and 30) will reveal
that the total value of all goods and services produced in the Charleston
study area during 1968 amounted to $2.232 billion. Of this amount,
$835 million were sold outside the region—that is, $835 million flowed
into the region during 1968. Table 6 illustrates the direct and indirect
relationship between external sales and the total value of goods produced in the Charleston study area. Sector 20 (Other Wholesale and
Retail Trade), for example, had external sales amounting to $96,108,000.
These sales generated an additional $57,405,000 in internal sales, so.
that the total direct and indirect income resulting from "Other Wholesale and Retail Trade" activity in 1968 was $153,513,000 ($96,108,000
times 1.6973, the multiplier). "Other Wholesale and Retail Trade,"
therefore, accounted for approximately 7.6 percent of the total economic
output of the Charleston area in 1968.

A brief summary of the local Charleston economy by major
economic sectors is given in Table 6. The table shows the importance,

---

*There is an important distinction that must be made between
the technical and interdependence coefficients with respect to sales.
The technical coefficients refer to a change of $1 in the production
of output of the endogenous sector regardless of whether it goes to
final demand or is used locally. The interdependence coefficients
refer to a dollar change in final demand only.

TABLE 6

Direct and Indirect Shares of Total Revenues Generated by Sectors,
Charleston Study Area, 1968

	External Sales ($1,000)	External Sales Multiplier	Total Direct and Indirect Value ($1,000)	Percent Share of Total Revenue ($1,000)
1. Agriculture, Forestry, & Fisheries	3,341	3.1636	10,570	0.52
2. Food & Kindred Products	6,565	2.9478	19,352	0.95
3. Construction & Mining	12,685	3.7922	48,104	2.37
4. Textiles & Apparel Manufacturing	1,196	3.0983	3,706	0.18
5. Lumber, Pulp, & Paper Prods.	77,637	1.9027	147,720	7.28
6. Furniture & Fixtures Mfg.	1,282	2.9934	3,838	0.18
7. Printers & Publishers	9	3.1712	28	0
8. Chemical Manufacturing	2,533	2.3837	6,038	0.29
9. Petroleum & Coal Mfg.	208	2.6418	549	0.02
10. Rubber, Plastic, & Related	938	2.7961	2,623	0.12
11. Stone, Clay, & Glass Prods. Mfg.	1,144	3.2726	3,744	0.18
12. Machinery, Repairs, & Metal Shops	20,608	3.0452	62,755	3.09
13. Miscellaneous Manufacturing	7	2.2331	16	0
14. Transportation	12,905	3.1079	40,107	1.97
15. Communications	9	2.3065	21	0
16. Utilities	12,723	2.4069	30,623	1.50
17. Eating & Drinking Places	18,407	1.5540	28,604	1.40
18. Hotels & Lodging Places	12,232	2.7808	34,015	1.67
19. Gasoline Service Stations	24,204	2.4865	60,183	2.96
20. Other Wholesale & Retail Trade	96,108	1.6973	153,513	7.56
21. Finance & Insurance	4	2.9635	12	0
22. Real Estate	25	4.4798	112	0
23. Other Business & Professional Services	87	3.3003	287	0.01
24. Local & State Government	41,920	3.3436	140,163	6.90
25. Defense-Related Government	347,718	3.1659	1,100,840	54.25
26. Other Federal Government	25,368	3.2153	81,566	4.01
27. Households	21,117	2.2534	47,585	2.34
28. Unallocated	1,221	1.9225	2,347	0.11
	742,201*		1,029,021*	99.86

*Figure not equal to Table 1 totals due to rounding errors.

<u>Source:</u> Calculated using data in Tables 3 and 5.

81

in terms of economic activity generated through external sales, of each of the various sectors. For example, federal government sectors generated 54 percent (by far the major portion) of the total economic activities in the Charleston study area.

ALTERNATIVE APPROACHES TO INPUT-OUTPUT MODELS

The procedure discussed in this chapter for developing an input-output model is only one of several possible methods that may be employed. Basically, there are two main approaches to regional input-output analysis: (1) national coefficients and (2) primary data. The use of national coefficients on a regional basis has several inherent problems. For example, the variations in "industry mix" and "product mix" by regions means that the regional interindustry flows will be in error to the extent that the region's industry and product composition differs from that of the nation. On the other hand, models based on empirical approaches face tremendous quantity-of-data problems. The collection of data is difficult, costly, and time consuming. At the beginning of this chapter are listed various common sources of regional input-output methodology which deal with these problems as well as illustrating for synthesizing the two approaches. However, it is felt that, for planning purposes, especially as related to small local economies, two other approaches merit discussion.

The first approach employs the use of location quotients to build a regional input-output model from the national input-output table.[10] The location quotient is basically a device for comparing a region's percentage share of a particular activity with its percentage share of the national activity.[11] In other words, it compares the relative importance of an industry in a region to its relative importance in the nation. Essentially, the procedure is as follows: If a region's location quotient is greater than one for an activity, it is assumed that the region produces more than enough to meet local needs for that activity, no imports are needed, and that the excess production is exported. If the location quotient is less than one, the opposite would be assumed. If the region's location quotient for an activity is just equal to one, it is assumed that the region just satisfies local needs for that activity and that no imports or exports are made. Interregional flows are calculated by taking national flows of an activity and weighting them by the relative sizes of the local purchasing industries.

Unfortunately, the location quotient model is not adequate, in and of itself, for planning purposes. However, it does provide a starting point. The data generated may be used for sectors not considered essential to the study. This allows the researcher to concentrate the time and budget allocated for the study to collecting primary data in sectors considered to be of major importance. An example of this could be a study concerned with estimating the economic impact of activities that by their very nature require a coastal location. Sectors such as naval installations, ship and boat building, marinas, commercial fisheries, etc., could be developed in great detail from field surveys, while the location quotient model could be used to generate data for such sectors as agriculture, utilities, or medical services, which may not be considered of primary importance to the study.

Though this approach has the obvious difficulty of fitting the secondary and the empirical data into a unified table, this difficulty seems no worse than the one involved in other methods using both types of information.

Another approach to the simulation of regional input-output tables has been suggested by Professor Leontief and Alan Strout. This approach is based on the use of a gravity trade model for estimation of interregional commodity flows.[12] The basic premise of the gravity model is that trade between two regions is a direct function of the number of potential customers in one region, the number of potential suppliers in the other, and an inverse function of the distance between the two regions. Professor Karen Polenske of Harvard has undertaken a testing of the Leontief-Strout model using as a base the empirically derived mine-region, interregional 1960 input-output table for Japan. She found that the gravity trade model gave reasonably good estimates of the actual flows as indicated by empirical data.[13] Though this procedure is more complicated than the location quotient approach, it appears to provide more adequate estimates. Consequently, the Leontief-Strout, or gravity model, approach is another viable alternative for simulating a regional input-output table and, thus, a possible means of avoiding the expense and time associated with the construction of a table primarily from survey information.

NOTES

1. Walter Isard, "Interregional and Regional Input-Output Analysis: A Model of a Space Economy," The Review of Economics and Statistics, XXXIII (1951), 318-28; Hollis B. Chenery and Paul G. Clark, Interindustry Analysis (New York: Wiley and Sons, 1959);

William H. Miernyk, The Elements of Input-Output Analysis (New York: Random House, 1965); W. W. Leontief, ed., Input-Output Economics, (New York: Oxford University Press, 1966).

2. F. T. Moore and J. W. Peterson, "Regional Analysis: An Interindustry Model of Utah," Review of Economics and Statistics, XXXVII (1955), 368-83; Hays B. Gamble and David L. Raphael, A Microregional Analysis of Clinton County Pennsylvania Vols. 1 and 2 (University Park: The Pennsylvania Regional Analysis Group, Pennsylvania State University, 1965); Charles Tiebout, "Regional and Interregional Input-Output Models: An Appraisal," The Southern Economic Journal, XXIV (1957), 140-47; L. N. Moses, "The Stability of Interregional Trading Patterns in Input-Output Analysis," American Economic Review, XLV (1955), 803-32; W. Z. Hirsch, "Interindustry Relations of a Metropolitan Area," Review of Economics and Statistics, XLI (1959), 360-69; H. C. Davis, Economic Evaluation of Water, Part V: Multiregional Input-Output Techniques and Western Water Resource Development, Water Resources Center Contribution No. 125, Sanitary Engineering Research Lab, University of California, Berkeley, 1968.

3. For an explanation of export base theory, see George Hildebrand and George Mace, Jr., "The Empirical Multiplier in an Expanding Industrial Market: Los Angeles County, 1940-1947," Review of Economics and Statistics, XXXII (1950), 241-49.

4. See Charles M. Tiebout, "Exports and Regional Economic Growth," Journal of Political Economy, LXIV (1956), 160-64; also a reply by Douglas C. North, same issue, 165-68.

5. J. R. Meyer, "Regional Economics: A Survey," American Economic Review, LIII (1963), 19-54.

6. Robert L. Canion and Warren L. Trock, Input-Output as a Method of Evaluation of the Economic Impact of Water, Water Resources Institute, Technical Report No. 12, Texas A&M University, College Station, May, 1968.

7. Gamble and Raphael, p. 24.

8. "Sales Management Survey of Buying Power 1969," Sales Management Magazine, June, 1969.

9. "1967 Census of Manufactures: Preliminary Report," South Carolina, Bureau of the Census, United States Department of Commerce, Washington, D.C., February, 1970.

10. William A. Schaffer and Kong Chu, "Simulating Regional Interindustry Models for Western States," paper presented at the Pacific Regional Science Conference, Honolulu, Hawaii, August, 1969.

11. Walter Isard, Methods of Regional Analysis: An Introduction to Regional Science (Cambridge, Mass.: The MIT Press, 1960), p. 124.

12. Wassily Leontief and Alan Strout, "Multi-regional Input-Output Analysis," in Leontief, pp. 223-57.

13. Karen R. Polenske, "An Empirical Test of Interregional Input-Output Models: Estimation of 1963 Japanese Production," American Economic Review, May, 1970, 76-82.

7

EMPIRICAL EXAMINATION
OF
ECONOMIC-ECOLOGIC
LINKAGES

The model of economic-ecologic linkages developed in Chapter 3 contains two parts: (1) an input-output matrix of the pecuniary sectors of the economy and (2) an environmental matrix which shows the inputs (or outputs) of various natural resources (or pollutants) required to produce one dollar's worth of gross output by each sector in the input-output matrix. In the previous chapter, we have described how the input-output matrix for Charleston was constructed. In this chapter, we turn to the second part of the model-the environmental matrix—and we will examine how the two can be combined to produce meaningful empirical estimates of the direct and indirect linkages between the socioeconomic system and the environment of the Charleston area.

CONSTRUCTION OF THE ENVIRONMENTAL MATRIX

Basic Structure

The environmental matrix which has been constructed for the Charleston area is shown in Table 7. It contains twenty-eight columns—one for each of the endogenous sectors of the input-output matrix—and sixteen rows. Each of the sixteen rows represents either a natural resource input into the Charleston economy or an emission from the economy into the environment. Those coefficients which represent inputs are noted as positive numbers; those which represent emissions are noted as negative numbers. Some of the coefficients are in pounds per dollar of gross output, some are in gallons, and some are in acres, but the unit of measurement is noted in each row.

TABLE 7

Selected Natural Resource Inputs and Waste Emissions per $1 of Gross Output,
by Sector, Charleston Study Area, 1968

	Agriculture, Forestry, & Fisheries (1)	Food & Kindred Products (2)	Construction & Mining (3)	Textile & Apparel (4)	Lumber, Pulp, & Paper Prods. (5)	Furniture & Fixtures (6)	Printers & Publishers (7)
1. Particulates (lbs)	-.024000				-1.279000		
2. Hydrocarbons (lbs)							
3. Sulfur Dioxide (lbs)							
4. Gaseous Fluoride (lbs)							
5. Hydrogen Sulfide (lbs)					- .042000		
6. CO_2 (lb?)							
7. Aldehydes (lbs)							
8. NO_2 (lbs)							
9. Domestic Water (gals)		.000030	.000090	.000030	.000020	.000030	.000122
10. Cooling Water (gals)				.000350	.004910		
11. Process Water (gals)		.001490		.003030	.014700		
12. Total Water Intake (gals)		.001520		.003410	.019630		
13. Discharge (gals)		-.001490		-.002890	- .147000		
14. Five-Day BOD (lbs)		-.326400		-.383400	-1.350100		
15. Suspended Solids (lbs)				-.345000	- .994800		
16. Solid Waste (cu yds)			-.001090	-.000879	- .126050		

88

	Chemical Manufacturing (8)	Petroleum & Coal Mfg. (9)	Rubber, Plastic, & Related Mfg. (10)	Stone, Clay, & Glass Prods. Mfg. (11)	Machinery, Repairs, & Metal Shops (12)	Miscellaneous Manufacturing (13)	Transportation (14)	Communications (15)
1.		-6.500000		-.920000	-.539600		-.021330	
2.		-5.026500					-.006000	
3.								
4.								
5.								
6.	.020670						-.020670	
7.	.002400						-.002400	
8.							-.014000	
9.	.000030	.000523	.000026		.000016			
10.	.000650	.000650	.000667		.001600			
11.	.008200	.000208						
12.	.001500	.001381	.000694	.001533	.001624			
13.	-.000870	-.001206	-.000654	-.001533				
14.	-.106200	-.000007			-.000008			
15.	-.053100			-.000005				
16.	-.000550	-.000712		-.000550	-.000550		-.000012	-.000566

(continued)

(Table 7, continued)

	Utilities (16)	Eating & Drinking Places (17)	Hotels & Lodging Places (18)	Gasoline Service Stations* (19)	Other Wholesale & Retail Trade (20)	Finance & Insurance (21)	Real Estate (22)	Other Bus. & Professional Services (23)
1.	-.011919			-.034000				
2.	-.003814			-.647000				
3.	-.374270			-.003000				
4.								
5.								
6.	-.000048			-.704300				
7.	-.000715			-.011000				
8.	-.123961							
9.								
10.								
11.								
12.								
13.								
14.								
15.								
16.	-.004300	-.003787	-.004491	-.000176				

	Local & State Government (24)	Defense-Related Government (25)	Other Federal Government (26)	Households* (27)	Unallocated (28)
1.					
2.					
3.					
4.					
5.					
6.					
7.					
8.					14.700000
9.					
10.					
11.					14.700000
12.					-14.700000
13.					- .241310
14.					
15.					- .008445
16.	-.000016	-.000160	-.000510		

*Emissions of automobiles are charged to gasoline service stations rather than to households.

Sources: R. L. Duprey, Compilation of Air Pollutant Emission Factors, U.S. Department of Health, Education and Welfare Public Health Service, National Air Pollution Control Administration, Durham, N.C., Public Health Service Publication No. 999-AP-42, 1968; James M. Stepp, Water Use, Waste Treatment, Water Pollution and Related Economic Data on South Carolina Manufacturing Plants, Water Resources Research Institute, Clemson University, Clemson, S.C., Report No. 8, August, 1968; Walter Isard and Eliahu Romanoff, unpublished water use and water pollution coeffi-cients, Regional Science Research Institute, Cambridge, Mass., 1967; marshland coefficients are derived from personal interviews with officials of Charleston District, U.S. Army Corps of Engineers; solid waste coefficients are derived from survey data, Charleston Area Input-Output Study, 1969.

Source of Data

The data for use in computing the coefficients shown in the matrix in Table 7 were obtained from numerous sources. Each of the firms surveyed in the collection of the input-output data was also asked to answer a series of questions concerning natural resource usage and waste disposal. Specific information was obtained from this survey as to usage of fresh and brackish water, output of liquid waste in pounds of BOD, and solid waste output. However, many firms which responded to the questionnaire did not answer one or more of the environmental linkages questions and the data obtained from the survey is of rather uneven quality. Consequently, the survey data was heavily supplemented by data obtained from two published works. For air pollution data, much engineering information was obtained from Duprey.[1] A survey of manufacturing plants in South Carolina by Stepp was found to be quite useful as a source of data on water use and liquid waste.[2] The data obtained from these two sources were further supplemented by unpublished data collected in the Boston and Philadelphia areas by Walter Isard and Eliahu Romanoff and by personal interviews. Like the coefficients in the input-output matrix, all data are based on best estimates for existing, in-place technology.

A critical examination of Table 7 will reveal that there is little or no data in many sectors which one would expect to have important linkages to the environment. For example, "Construction and Mining," which includes land and gravel operations in the Charleston area, usually produces some particulate output in the form of dust particles. It was not possible, however, to obtain data for all sectors, either because the firms making up that sector did not report information in the survey, or there were no published sources at hand, or both. The blank cells in Table 7, therefore, do not necessarily imply that some sectors do not have ecologic linkages. Rather, they represent holes in our knowledge which must be filled by engineering and biological research. Nevertheless, because of those cases where these blank cells should have numbers, but presently do not, there will be a bias introduced into our estimates of the environmental impact of economic activities which will understate the impact.

The Aggregation Problem

In Chapter 3, we noted that some of the problems associated with the modified economic-ecologic linkages model proposed in this study arise from the aggregation of firms into economic sectors. That is, the waste of a dairy foods processing plant may be quite different from the waste of a bakery, yet they are both aggregated under the broad heading of "Food and Kindred Products." This aggregation problem becomes especially bothersome when one attempts to give the economic-ecologic model empirical content.

There are three possible, if not altogether satisfactory, solutions to the aggregation problem: (1) we can use a weighted average of the environmental coefficients, using gross output of the component types of firms making up the sector; (2) we can use mean survey data (which will be influenced by the mix of firms responding to the survey); or (3) we can build our input-output table at a very low level of aggregation—i.e., the four-digit (SIC) level. The third approach is probably most satisfactory, but such an input-output table is so large and difficult to manipulate as to be almost impractical. Consequently, we have used various combinations of the first two alternatives, depending upon whether the environmental data were derived from secondary sources or from the survey of Charleston area firms. The user of the model is cautioned that the coefficients in Table 7 are not appropriate for analysis of the environmental impact of the growth of highly specialized firms within a particular sector.

Assumptions Underlying Environmental Coefficients

Since almost all the coefficients in the environmental matrix in Table 7 had to be imputed from other data, it was necessary to make certain assumptions to perform the calculation. The most important of these from a conceptual approach, perhaps, was the assumption of linearity—that is, the structure of the input-output model requires that we assume the same amount of natural resource usage or environmental emission per $1 of gross output will occur at $1 of gross output or at $1 million of gross output. Undoubtedly, this assumption of linearity with regard to environmental linkages is not realistic, and, in some cases, the assumption may cause serious problems. For example, we would hardly expect miles of automobile use to increase proportionately with household income, and, consequently, exhaust emissions from private households will not be a linear function of gross household income. To minimize the problems arising from the assumption of linearity, coefficients related to private automobile exhaust emissions were charged to "Gasoline Service Stations" rather than households on the premise that exhaust emissions are much more likely to be linearly associated with gasoline sales than household income. By the same token, emissions resulting from space heating of private homes are charged to "Utilities," rather than to households. In general, the convention was to charge a linkage to the sector where linearity was most likely to be realistic, rather than to the actual sector directly responsible.

Another assumption which affected the coefficients in Table 7 was necessitated by the fact that much of the available data was in engineering terms. Duprey's compilation of air pollutant emissions is based on physical units rather than dollar output. Consequently, in order to use these data within the format of the model, it was necessary to assume prices for the physical units of capital. The basic source for such prices was 1969 Business Statistics.[3] This price information was supplemented by telephone checks with the sales offices of leading manufacturers.

The data collected by Stepp required a special assumption before they could be utilized in the format required for this study. Stepp's data is reported on a "per employee" basis, rather than a dollar output or physical output basis. Transformation of the data from Professor Stepp's survey required, therefore, use of estimates of output per employee. The estimates used to make these transformations were obtained from unpublished data prepared for the Water Resources Council by the Regional Economics Division, Office of Business Economics, U.S. Department of Commerce. These data include 1960 and 1970 estimates of output per worker for major manufacturing industries in each of the OBE economic subareas of the United States, one of which is centered on Charleston County. Estimates of output per worker for 1968 were obtained by interpolation.

There were other assumptions of a less general nature which are difficult to enumerate. For example, households were assumed to drive each automobile owned about 10,000 miles per year locally. Commercial truck transportation was allocated between local and long-distance hauls based on information obtained from the 1967 Census of Transportation.[4]

All the coefficients should be considered as only first approximations. The model is flexible enough, however, that these coefficients can be revised and improved as our knowledge increases, and the model can serve the useful purpose of stimulating the research needed to improve these coefficients.

MATING THE INPUT-OUTPUT AND ENVIRONMENTAL MATRIXES

In Chapter 3, we described how an input-output matrix and an environmental matrix might be mated to generate estimates of the direct and indirect environmental impact of specific changes in economic output. Before this mating can actually take place, however, we must make some specific modifications in the Charleston input-output model.

We have characterized the Charleston input-output model as being "closed" with respect to the government sectors. That is, state and local, defense-related federal, and nondefense federal government sectors are considered as endogenous parts of the Charleston economy. For many purposes, it is useful to close in the government sectors, but the consequence of doing so is that changes in the level of non-government activities at Charleston will automatically induce changes in the level of all three types of government activities at Charleston. These induced effects on government result from consideration of taxes paid to government sectors as purchases from government.

There can be little question that increases or decreases in taxes paid by Charleston firms to local and state government, resulting from increases or decreases in the level of local, nongovernmental economic activities, will probably induce changes in the level of state and local governmental spending. There is much more room to question, however, whether changes in the taxes paid by Charleston area firms to the federal government will have any important effect on federal activities in the area. Hence, the use of tax data in the two federal government rows may result in the input-output model generating greater induced effects for any given economic change than would be, in fact, realized. Since the federal government sectors have some significant environmental linkages, the consequence would be an overestimation of the environmental impact associated with certain changes in the economic activity of nongovernment sectors.

Our problem, therefore, is to modify the model so as to eliminate the induced effects on the federal government sectors without elimina-ting the federal government's induced effects on the remainder of the local economy. We want to retain the two federal sectors' columns within the endogenous matrix, but eliminate the two federal sectors' rows. If we eliminate the rows altogether, however, we will no longer have a square matrix and we will not be able to obtain the Leontief inverse necessary to implement the economic-ecologic linkages model. Our solution is to block out the two federal government rows— to assume all numbers in those two rows to be zero. This solution gives us the desired results in that the nongovernmental sectors do not induce any indirect effects on federal activity, but federal activity does induce secondary effects on the nonfederal sectors. Therefore, before the input-output matrix and the environmental matrix were mated, rows 26 and 27 were reduced to zero.

WASTE TREATMENT POSSIBILITIES

The environmental matrix in Table 7 is based on estimates of current intakes or discharges. One perhaps should have several such matrixes based on assumptions of no treatment and several different levels of treatment, but such data appear to be very difficult to obtain because, in any given locale (such as the Charleston area), there are considerable differences prevailing in the level of treatment. In some sectors, waste is treated to fairly high levels before discharge; in others, there is practically no treatment. At best, firms only have information on their actual waste discharges, and they can only surmise the discharge levels which would prevail under alternative waste treatment operations.

The input-output table itself and the assumptions of static technology which it requires also pose a problem to the incorporation of waste treatment possibilities into the environmental matrix. Each column in the input-output table indicates the current purchases of the firms in that sector, given the in-place technical processes. Even if it were practical to build environmental matrixes for alternative levels of treatment, we would create problems in mating these matrixes with an input-output matrix based on current practices because alternative treatment levels necessitate changes in the purchasing patterns of the various industrial sectors.

Ideally, one would desire various sets of input-output and environmental matrixes based on alternative treatment levels for each of the types of discharges. If such were available, we could then use the technique of comparative statics to analyze the economic and environmental effects of not only changing the level of economic activity, but also of changing the level of treatment. At present, we do not have the extensive data which this ideal solution requires. We shall confine our empirical analysis of economic-ecologic linkages in the Charleston area to observations on changes in the level of various economic activities on the pecuniary income and environment of the area.

DIRECT AND INDIRECT ENVIRONMENTAL IMPACTS

The data in Table 8 were obtained by postmultiplying the environmental matrix (Table 7) by the Leontief inverse of the Charleston

TABLE 8

Direct and Indirect Environmental Impacts of $1 Increase in External Deliveries, by Sector, Charleston Study Area, 1968

	Agriculture, Forestry, & Fisheries (1)	Food & Kindred Products (2)	Construction & Mining (3)	Textile & Apparel (4)	Lumber, Paper, & Pulp (5)	Furniture & Fixtures Mfg. (6)	Printers & Publishers (7)
1. Particulates (lbs)	.0512	.0268	.0837	.0193	1.3028	.6742	.1888
2. Hydrocarbons (lbs)	.0325	.0277	.0155	.0210	.0125	.0445	.0206
3. Sulfur Dioxide (lbs)	.0103	.0159	.0215	.0111	.0215	.0429	.0273
4. Gaseous Florides (lbs)	.0006	.0012	.0028	.0008	.0031	.0019	.0036
5. Hydrogen Sulfide (lbs)	.0003	.0003	.0023	.0003	.0431	.0218	.0003
6. CO_2 (lbs)	.0265	.0016	.0109	.0147	.0071	.0116	.0145
7. Aldehydes (lbs)	.0005	.0003	.0002	.0003	.0002	.0003	.0003
8. NO_2 (lbs)	.0025	.0030	.0018	.0023	.0015	.0107	.0021
9. Domestic Water (gals)	10.2799	10.1591	9.4256	12.7709	5.0273	9.7076	12.7799
10. Cooling Water (gals)	0	0	.0003	.0004	.0051	.0026	0
11. Process Water (gals)	.0001	.0018	.0009	.0032	.0151	.0076	.0002
12. Total Water Intake (gals)	10.2768	10.1609	9.4267	12.7742	5.0475	9.7178	12.7991
13. Total Water Discharge (gals)	10.2768	10.1609	9.4263	12.7736	5.0424	9.7152	12.7990
14. Five-Day BOD (lbs)	.1853	.5519	.2367	.6150	1.4714	.8640	.2289
15. Suspended Solids (lbs)	.0094	.0114	.0648	.3601	1.0303	.5218	.0201
16. Solid Waste (cu yds)	.0072	.0073	.0158	.0098	.1333	.0720	.0098

(continued)

97

(Table 8, continued)

	Chemical Manufacturing (8)	Petroleum & Coal Mfg. (9)	Rubber, Plastic, & Related Mfg. (10)	Stone, Clay, & Glass Prods. Mfg. (11)	Machinery & Metal Shops (12)	Miscellaneous Manufacturing (13)	Transportation (14)	Communications (15)
1.	.0167	6.5207	.0159	.9463	.5928	.2208	.0441	.0136
2.	.0131	5.0433	.0166	.0226	.0372	.0184	.0332	.0175
3.	1.0443	.0576	.2361	.0341	.0225	.0188	.0094	.0082
4.	.1758	.0089	.0391	.0047	.0009	.0016	.0005	.0003
5.	.0004	.0005	.0003	.0005	.0006	.0005	.0004	.0002
6.	.0094	.0125	.0123	.0171	.0129	.0091	.0427	.0110
7.	.0002	.0002	.0002	.0003	.0003	.0002	.0029	.0002
8.	.0017	.0016	.0017	.0021	.0058	.0032	.0168	.0022
9.	7.0076	11.1113	10.7823	15.2843	11.5069	8.1329	14.7890	8.5504
10.	.0008	.0007	.0009	0	.0017	0	.0001	0
11.	.0010	.0004	.0003	.0002	.0003	.0002	.0002	.0001
12.	7.0094	11.1249	10.7835	15.2862	11.5088	8.1333	14.7893	8.5506
13.	7.0086	11.1122	10.7832	15.2861	11.5071	8.1332	14.7892	8.5502
14.	.2459	.2080	.2170	.2779	.2153	.1576	.2625	.1520
15.	.5853	.0405	.1357	.0288	.0186	.0193	.0116	.0069
16.	.0659	.0117	.0208	.0125	.0101	.0070	.0102	.0065

	Utilities (16)	Eating & Drinking Places (17)	Hotels & Lodging Places (18)	Gasoline Service Stations (19)	Other Wholesale & Retail Trade (20)	Finance & Insurance (21)	Real Estate (22)	Other Bus. & Professional Services (23)
1.	.0533	.0142	.0231	.0682	.0084	.0199	.0706	.0234
2.	.3961	.0315	.0311	.6767	.0084	.0151	.0157	.0239
3.	.3828	.0251	.0192	.0093	.0066	.0085	.0211	.0260
4.	.0005	.0004	.0007	.0007	.0004	.0007	.0027	.0023
5.	.0003	.0002	.0003	.0002	.0002	.0004	.0019	.0004
6.	.0087	.0078	.0111	.7119	.0040	.0111	.0106	.0107
7.	.0009	.0002	.0002	.0111	.0001	.0002	.0002	.0002
8.	.1259	.0076	.0051	.0015	.0016	.0015	.0019	.0043
9.	7.4750	6.2092	9.6079	5.5242	3.0781	9.7889	9.1126	7.9100
10.	0	0	0	0	0	0	.0003	0
11.	.0001	.0003	.0002	.0001	0	.0002	.0007	.0002
12.	7.4752	6.2095	9.6082	5.5243	3.0783	9.7891	9.1135	7.9103
13.	7.4751	6.2095	9.6082	5.5243	3.0783	9.7890	9.1132	7.9102
14.	.1370	.1611	.0869	.1033	.0629	.1799	.2192	.1537
15.	.0091	.0062	.0096	.0067	.0056	.0132	.0553	.0191
16.	.0100	.0085	.0114	.0042	.0025	.0075	.0140	.0070

(continued)

99

(Table 8, continued)

	Local & State Government (24)	Defense-Related Government (25)	Other Federal Government (26)	Households (27)	Unallocated (28)
1.	.0460	.0247	.0325	.0227	.0204
2.	.0418	.0246	.0293	.0256	.0078
3.	.0133	.0104	.0150	.0092	.0044
4.	.0009	.0006	.0009	.0005	.0005
5.	.0005	.0005	.0005	.0004	.0004
6.	.0197	.0176	.0164	.0197	.0021
7.	.0004	.0003	.0003	.0003	0
8.	.0029	.0024	.0034	.0023	.0004
9.	15.8805	15.8231	14.4777	17.7191	1.7695
10.	0	0	0	0	.0005
11.	.0002	.0002	.0002	.0002	.0002
12.	15.8808	15.8233	14.4779	17.7193	1.7662
13.	15.8807	15.8232	14.4779	17.7192	1.7661
14.	.2848	.2814	.2616	.3111	.0435
15.	.0155	.0132	.0160	.0114	.0115
16.	.0113	.0112	.0112	.0119	.0028

Source: Calculated using data in Tables 5 and 7.

100

input-output matrix (Table 5).* These data show the direct and indirect changes in environmental usage and discharges into the ambient environment resulting from an increase of $1 in the external sales (or sales to buyers outside the Charleston area) of each of the twenty-eight sectors in the input-output table. External sales must be interpreted very broadly as pecuniary inflows into the Charleston area, either for goods or services actually exported to other areas, or in the form of tax monies for the operation of government agencies or in the form of transfer payments, such as social security payments to households.

One of the most striking features of Table 8 to many readers will be the presence of numbers in every cell. Even those sectors which did not show a direct ecologic linkage in Table 7 show a linkage in Table 8. All sectors show either a direct or indirect linkage (or both) in Table 8. This results from the economic interdependence demonstrated in the Leontief inverse of the input-output table. While a sector may not directly emit particulates into the area, its external sale may indirectly cause particulate pollution because it purchases inputs from sectors which do emit particulates. Thus, Table 8 shows that all sectors do, in fact, have ecologic linkages—all, either directly or indirectly, are responsible for some level of pollution.

On the basis of the preliminary data used in implementing this model, we can identify some of the sectors where major environmental impacts are associated with changes in the level of economic activity. For example, the "Petroleum and Coal" sector appears to be the major emitter of particulates into the atmosphere; Table 8 shows that 6.5207 pounds of particulates are emitted as the result of $1 of external sales by that industry. The "Lumber, Pulp, and Paper" sector also has a high level of particulate emissions—1.3028 pounds per dollar of external sales. "Petroleum and Coal" is also a major emitter of hydrocarbons—5.0433 pounds per dollar of external sales.

Since we are concerned specifically with the resources of the coastal zone, discharges of water pollutants are of special interest. Table 8 shows that "Lumber, Pulp, and Paper" is also a major factor in discharge of "BOD" and "Suspended Solids" into the waters. Direct and indirect "Five-Day BOD" discharges resulting from $1 of external sales by that industry are 1.4714 pounds and "Suspended Solids"

---

*Signs have been ignored since, in this case, they seemed to be mathematically pendantic.

TABLE 9

Direct and Indirect Environmental Emissions per $1 of Local Pecuniary Income
Generated, Charleston Study Area, 1968

	Agriculture, Forestry, & Fisheries (1)	Food & Kindred Products (2)	Construction & Mining (3)	Textile & Apparel (4)	Lumber & Wood Products (5)	Furniture & Fixtures Mfg. (6)	Printers & Publishers (7)
1. Particulates (lbs)	$ .0254	.0163	.0387	.0097	1.3090	.3883	.0894
2. Hydrocarbons (lbs)	.0161	.0168	.0072	.0106	.0124	.0256	.0098
3. Sulfur Dioxide (lbs)	.0051	.0097	.0099	.0056	.0213	.0247	.0129
4. Gaseous Fluorides (lbs)	.0003	.0007	.0013	.0004	.0031	.0011	.0017
5. Hydrogen Sulfide (lbs)	.0001	.0002	.0011	.0002	.0427	.0126	.0001
6. CO_2 (lbs)	.0131	.0010	.0050	.0074	.0070	.0067	.0069
7. Aldehydes (lbs)	.0002	.0002	.0001	.0002	.0002	.0002	.0001
8. NO_2 (lbs)	.0012	.0018	.0008	.0012	.0015	.0062	.0010
9. Domestic Water (gals)	5.0999	6.1885	4.3566	2.0765	4.9820	5.5916	6.0513
10. Cooling Water (gals)	.0000	.0000	.0001	.0002	.0057	.0015	.0000
11. Process Water (gals)	.0000	.0011	.0004	.0016	.0150	.0044	.0001
12. Total Water Intake (gals)	5.0983	6.4626	4.3572	2.0766	5.0021	5.5974	6.0604
13. Total Water Discharge (gals)	5.0983	6.4626	4.3571	2.0762	4.9971	5.5960	6.0603
14. Five-Day BOD (lbs)	.0919	.3369	.1094	.3097	1.4581	.4977	.1084
15. Suspended Solids (lbs)	.0047	.0069	.0300	.1814	1.0210	.3006	.0095
16. Solid Waste (cu yds)	.0036	.0044	.0073	.0049	.1321	.0415	.0046

	Chemical Manufacturing (8)	Petroleum & Coal Mfg. (9)	Rubber, Plastic, & Related Mfg. (10)	Stone, Clay, & Glass Prods. Mfg. (11)	Machinery, Repairs, & Metal Shops (12)	Miscellaneous Manufacturing (13)	Transportation (14)	Communications (15)
1.	$ .0113	4.2930	.0089	.4190	.3112	.1628	.0196	.0089
2.	.0089	3.2817	.0092	.0100	.0195	.0136	.0147	.0114
3.	.7122	.0375	.1317	.0151	.0118	.0138	.0042	.0054
4.	.1199	.0058	.0218	.0021	.0005	.0012	.0002	.0002
5.	.0003	.0003	.0002	.0002	.0003	.0004	.0002	.0001
6.	.0064	.0081	.0069	.0076	.0068	.0067	.0190	.0072
7.	.0001	.0001	.0001	.0001	.0002	.0001	.0013	.0001
8.	.0012	.0010	.0009	.0009	.0030	.0024	.0075	.0014
9.	4.7792	7.2301	6.0133	6.7679	6.0400	5.9956	6.5678	5.5920
10.	.0005	.0004	.0005	.0000	.0009	.0000	.0000	.0000
11.	.0007	.0003	.0002	.0001	.0002	.0001	.0001	.0001
12.	4.7804	7.2390	6.0140	6.7687	6.0410	5.9959	6.5679	5.5921
13.	4.7799	7.2390	6.0138	6.7687	6.0401	5.9958	6.5679	5.5918
14.	.1672	.1353	.1210	.1231	.1130	.1162	.1166	.0994
15.	.3992	.0264	.0757	.0128	.0098	.0142	.0052	.0045
16.	.0449	.0076	.0116	.0055	.0053	.0052	.0045	.0043

(continued)

(Table 9, continued)

	Utilities (16)	Eating & Drinking Places (17)	Hotels & Lodging Places (18)	Gasoline Service Stations (19)	Other Wholesale & Retail Trade (20)	Finance & Insurance (21)	Real Estate (22)	Other Bus. & Professional Services (23)
1.	$ .0334	.0086	.0113	.0434	.0072	.0100	.0257	.0113
2.	.2479	.0190	.0152	.4308	.0072	.0076	.0057	.0116
3.	.2396	.0151	.0094	.0059	.0056	.0043	.0077	.0126
4.	.0003	.0002	.0003	.0004	.0003	.0004	.0010	.0011
5.	.0002	.0001	.0001	.0001	.0002	.0002	.0007	.0002
6.	.0054	.0047	.0054	.4532	.0034	.0056	.0039	.0052
7.	.0006	.0001	.0001	.0071	.0001	.0001	.0001	.0001
8.	.0788	.0046	.0025	.0010	.0014	.0008	.0007	.0021
9.	4.6786	3.7429	4.6886	3.5167	2.6269	4.9170	3.3197	3.8253
10.	.0000	.0000	.0000	.0000	.0000	.0000	.0001	.0000
11.	.0001	.0002	.0001	.0001	.0000	.0001	.0002	.0001
12.	4.6787	3.7431	4.6888	3.5168	2.6270	4.9171	3.3200	3.8254
13.	4.6787	3.7431	4.6888	3.5168	2.6270	4.9170	3.3199	3.8254
14.	4.0857	.0971	.0912	.0658	.0537	.0904	.0798	.0743
15.	.0057	.0037	.0047	.0043	.0048	.0066	.0201	.0092
16.	.0063	.0051	.0056	.0027	.0021	.0038	.0051	.0034

	Local & State Government (24)	Defense-Related Government (25)	Other Federal Government (26)	Households (27)	Unallocated (28)
1.	$ .0162	.0141	.0190	.0121	.0215
2.	.0148	.0141	.0171	.0137	.0082
3.	.0047	.0060	.0088	.0049	.0046
4.	.0003	.0003	.0005	.0003	.0005
5.	.0002	.0003	.0003	.0002	.0004
6.	.0070	.0101	.0096	.0105	.0022
7.	.0001	.0002	.0002	.0002	.0000
8.	.0010	.0014	.0020	.0012	.0004
9.	5.6122	9.0571	8.4593	9.4655	1.8681
10.	.0000	.0000	.0000	.0000	.0005
11.	.0001	.0001	.0001	.0001	.0002
12.	5.6123	9.0572	8.4594	9.4656	1.8646
13.	5.6123	9.0572	8.4594	9.4656	1.8646
14.	.1006	.1611	.1528	.1662	.0459
15.	.0055	.0076	.0093	.0061	.0121
16.	.0040	.0064	.0065	.0064	.0030

Source: Calculated by using data in Table 8 and Appendix Table 2.

discharges are 1.0303 pounds. No other sector comes close to those levels; the next highest sector in BOD discharges is "Furniture and Fixtures" with .8640 pounds and the next highest sector in "Suspended Solids" discharge is "Chemicals" with .5853 pounds.

ENVIRONMENTAL IMPACTS AND PECUNIARY INCOME

The Leontief inverse of the input-output matrix allows us to compute local sales multipliers showing the total (direct plus indirect) effects an area sales of a $1 change in deliveries to final demand from any sector. These numbers are calculated by summing each column in the Leontief inverse shown in Table 5. If we multiply all the numbers in each row in the Leontief inverse by an appropriate value-added coefficient, however, we can also calculate local income multipliers in the same way. These local income multipliers show the effect on Charleston area income of a $1 change in deliveries to final demand from any given sector. The value-added coefficients and transformed income matrix are included as Appendix Tables 1 and 2. We can use the local income multipliers to reformulate the information in the matrix shown in Table 8 into a new matrix which shows the direct and indirect environmental impacts per dollar of local pecuniary income of each sector in the input-output table. This new matrix is presented in Table 9.

Table 9 shows that particulate and hydrocarbon emissions from "Petroleum and Coal" continue to be relatively high, even when computed on the basis of local income generated. The emissions from "Lumber, Pulp, and Paper" are also relatively high. The "BOD" and "Suspended Solids" discharge of "Lumber, Pulp, and Paper" are also relatively high.

EVALUATING THE LINKAGES

Just as the structure of the Charleston area economy is unique, the indirect economic-ecologic linkages at Charleston are also unique. Other areas with a different economic base and a different industrial mix will have somewhat different indirect environmental impacts, even if the levels of waste treatment are exactly comparable to those at Charleston. And if the waste treatment levels were different, the resulting economic-ecologic linkages would be different as well. It is not valid, therefore, to generalize the Charleston linkages to other areas except in the crudest way.

We have warned that, while the data used to implement empirically this model of economic-ecologic linkages appear to be reasonable, they may not be highly accurate. It would be dangerous to draw any but the most tentative conclusions from the results presented in this chapter. We can see, however, that, even if the major environmental impacts are attributable to those commercial sectors which have direct and easily identifiable linkages to the ecosystem, the linkages are much more complex and far-reaching. The cumulative environmental impact of those sectors only indirectly linked to the ecosystem is quite significant. Evaluation of the direct linkages only will result in serious underestimation of the environmental impact of new industries in an area, or in the impact of growth in existing industries. The planner or resource manager who fails to note these indirect linkages will jeopardize the supply of environmental goods available to his community and create an economic problem of resource misallocation.

NOTES

1. R. L. Duprey, Compilation of Air Pollutant Emission Factors, U.S. Department of Health, Education and Welfare, Public Health Service, National Air Pollution Control Administration, Durham, N.C., Public Health Service Publication No. 999-AP-42, 1968.

2. James M. Stepp, Water Use, Waste Treatment, Water Pollution and Related Economic Data on South Carolina Manufacturing Plants, Water Resources Research Institute, Clemson University, Clemson, S.C., Report No. 8, August, 1968.

3. For example, for prices on paper products, see 1969 Business Statistics, 17th Biennial Edition, U.S. Department of Commerce, Office of Business Economics, Washington, D.C., 1969, p. 174.

4. U.S. Bureau of the Census, Census of Transportation, 1967, Truck Inventory and Use Survey, South Carolina (Washington, D.C.: U.S. Government Printing Office, July, 1968), pp. 6-7.

8

WILLINGNESS TO PAY
FOR
ENVIRONMENTAL
GOODS

In Chapter 4, we outlined an approach to ascertaining a rough measure of the demand price for environmental goods. This approach was based on the premise that value arises out of a willingness to pay, or a willingness to forego other opportunities, in order to obtain the environmental services of certain natural resources.

In this chapter, we will describe a pilot study designed to obtain willingness-to-pay information from households in the Charleston metropolitan area. This study does not represent a definitive effort. Rather, it can be viewed as a first, somewhat hesitant step which illustrates how the willingness-to-pay concept can be given empirical content and how empirical data might be analyzed for regional planning purposes.

DIFFICULTIES OF THE SURVEY TECHNIQUE

In Chapter 4, we noted that there were at least two possible approaches to ascertaining willingness to pay for a high-quality environment. One approach is to study the effects of air pollution, water pollution, etc., on property values. The other is more direct. It involves the use of a survey of a random sample of households. The latter approach has been chosen for the Charleston study.

Many of the difficulties associated with a household survey of willingness to pay for clean air and clean water can be anticipated on the basis of a priori reasoning. Ridker has enumerated three such difficulties:

(1) It is very difficult to phrase questions so that the interviewee understands and interprets them properly;

(2) The interviewee may not fully comprehend the hypothetical package of environmental goods about which he is being questioned (i.e., he has no point of reference in judging the value of goods which he has always considered free);

(3) There is no assurance that the interviewee would respond in a real situation in the same way he responds in the hypothetical situation posed by the enumerator.[1]

Nevertheless, household surveys have been used with some success in marketing research to obtain information not unlike that needed for ascertaining the economic value of environmental goods. Tests of the viability of the survey approach in providing willingness-to-pay data on environmental quality can be had only if pilot surveys are performed and evaluated. Accordingly, a small sample survey of households in the Charleston, South Carolina, area was undertaken in November, 1969.

SAMPLING PROCEDURE

The Charleston survey consisted of a random sampling of households in Charleston, Berkeley, and Dorchester counties. The sample was drawn in two stages. Within the incorporated limits of the city of Charleston, the sample was drawn by city blocks. Each city block was numbered and a random sample of blocks was selected. The enumerator was instructed to begin at the northwest corner of the block and work his way east, interviewing the household occupying every fourth dwelling unit. The unincorporated parts of Charleston, Berkeley, and Dorchester counties were divided into grids and each grid was numbered. Again, a random process was used to select grids and the enumerator was given the same formula for interviewing within the grid as within the city block. The sampling procedure resulted in a survey of 201 households. The estimated total number of households in the three counties in 1969 was 87,369; thus, the survey sampled only about 0.23 percent of the total households. Such a sample is quite small, but without a priori knowledge of the variance of the total population, one cannot estimate the proper sample size. One of the purposes of the pilot study is to obtain better estimates of the proper sample size for obtaining information on willingness to pay for environmental goods. Suffice it to say that, because of the small size of the sample, all results from this survey should be accepted with caution. Basic information about the size of the sample and the population is presented in Table 10.

The questions relating to willingness to pay for clean air and clean water were appended to a more general questionnaire designed to examine the buying patterns of Charleston area households for the input-output study. Respondents were asked to estimate the percentage of their gross annual household income which they would be willing to pay for four different levels of air and water quality. They were instructed to assume that the only way they could obtain these environmental goods was by purchasing them collectively with their neighbors. Thus, the responses were to be framed within the general context of joint and concurrent action by all members of the Charleston metropolitan area.

The four levels of environmental quality were specified in nontechnical concepts. Table 11 indicates how these quality levels were specified for both air and water. In addition, Table 11 also shows technical criteria which corresponds to the nontechnical specifications. The technical criteria for air quality is relatively straightforward, although there are certainly more parameters of air pollution than particulates and sulfur dioxide. In the case of water quality, however, technical criteria comparable to the nontechnical concepts are somewhat ambiguous. For example, the dissolved oxygen content of water may not be critical for swimming, yet it is certainly critical for fish life. By the same token, many factors can cause an unpleasant odor; e.g., water-organic materials in the water may break down, using up all the dissolved oxygen in the water and cause odor, or inorganic materials, such as hydrogen sulfide, may cause odor even in the presence of considerable dissolved oxygen in the water itself. Nevertheless, an attempt has been made in Table 11 to specify technical criteria which generally correspond to the nontechnical quality concepts used on the interview process.

In addition to information on willingness to pay, data were also obtained from each household on dollars of gross income from all sources in 1968 and on the locations of the household in the metropolitan area.

BIAS IN THE SURVEY

As a household survey, the Charleston metropolitan sample is probably biased against households in high-density areas and in favor of households in low-density areas. This bias is a result of the

TABLE 10

Sample Size, Estimated Household Number and Income,
by Household Income Class, Charleston Metropolitan Area, 1968

Household Income Class	Household Sample Size	Estimated Number Households[a]	Estimated Household Income[b]
Under $3,000	35	15,214	$ 22,821,000
3,000–5,999	43	18,692	84,114,000
6,000–8,999	44	19,129	143,467,500
9,000–11,999	35	15,214	159,747,000
12,000–14,999	20	8,695	117,382,500
15,000–17,999	13	5,645	93,142,500
18,000–20,999	8	3,478	67,821,000
Over $21,000	3	1,302	32,550,000
Totals	201	87,369	$721,045,500

[a]Calculated from Bureau of the Census, Current Population Reports, No. 2, p. 26.
[b]Sample survey of households.

112

TABLE 11

Nontechnical and Comparable Technical Specifications
of Four Levels of Air and Water Quality

Quality Level	Nontechnical Specification	Technical Criteria[a]
Air Quality I	No possible threat to health	80 μ g/m^3 particulates; 0.04 ppm SO$_2$
Air Quality II	No soiling of materials	60-180 μ g/m^3 particulates; 0.09 ppm SO$_2$
Air Quality III	No perceptible haze or smog	150 μ g/m^3 particulates; 0.10 ppm SO$_2$
Air Quality IV	No perceptible odor	[b] 0.06 ppm SO$_2$
Water Quality I	Clean enough to drink safely	DO>5 ppm; coilform<70/100 ml.
Water Quality II	Clean enough to swim safely	DO>5 ppm; coilform<70/100 ml.
Water Quality III	Clean enough to fish safely	DO>4 ppm; coilform<500/100 ml.
Water Quality IV	No unpleasant odor	DO>3 ppm

[a]Air standards obtained from Air Quality Criteria for Particulate Matter, National Air Pollution Control Administration, Publication No. AP-49, U.S. Public Health Service, Washington, D.C., January, 1969, pp. 188-89; and Air Quality Criteria for Sulfur Oxides, National Air Pollution Control Administration, Publication No. AP-50, U.S. Public Health Service, Washington, D.C. Water standards are for South Carolina, obtained from Water Quality Criteria, Addendum No. 1, State Water Pollution Control Board, State of California, Sacramento, 1954; Appendix EEE, pp. 127-29.
[b]Particulates are not normally associated with odor.

manner in which the random selection was made. The basic unit for
random choice was land area, and, unless the households were evenly
distributed across the land area of the metropolitan area, such a bias
could be expected. Some effort was made to correct against this bias
and to account for the clustering of households in the city of Charleston
itself by the use of city blocks as the basic random unit within the cor-
porate limits. The city blocks, on the average, are smaller in terms
of land area than the one-mile square grids used as the basic random
unit in the remainder of the metropolitan area, and, thus, use of these
city blocks had the effect of bending space in the high-density residence
zones. This adjustment was in the direction of making each random
unit roughly equal with regards to the number of households it contained.
Nevertheless, the adjustment was crude and some bias undoubtedly remains.

ENVIRONMENTAL QUALITY DATA
IN ZONE OF RESIDENCE

Although the Charleston metropolitan area is criss-crossed
with a number of fresh and brackish waterways and no residence zone
in the area is far removed from a body of water or marsh, there is no
body of data available in enough spatially specific detail to allow one
to assign an index of water quality to the particular residence zone
sampled in this survey. Consequently, it was decided that no test
could be made on the effect of water quality in the zone of residence
on a household's willingness to pay for water quality.

Data on suspended particulates and sulfur dioxide in the atmosphere were available, however. The South Carolina State Board of
Health has sampled for particulates at six points in Charleston County
over a number of years. The average number of particulate samples
for all points is 47, and the fewest number at any point is 17. Sampling
for sulfur dioxide has been under way at five points in Charleston
County, and average concentration information is available on a monthly
basis for thirty-seven consecutive months. The sampling points, both
for particulates and sulfur dioxide, are spread rather widely within
the high-density residence areas of Charleston County, and there is
little observable evidence of major pollution in other parts of the
metropolitan area.

Estimates of the concentration suspended particles and sulfur
dioxide in each of the sampled residence zones were made using a
generalized diffusion grid for the Charleston area developed by Purvis,
Kish, and Stromman.[2] These estimates are shown in Table 12. For

TABLE 12

Spatial Distribution of Atmospheric Particulate Pollution and Estimated Social
Awareness of Particulates by Sampling Zones, Charleston County, 1969

Area	Sampling Zone	Estimated Particulate Concentration ($\mu g/m^3$) [a]	Estimated Concentration of SO_2 (ppm)[b]
Charleston Proper	531	31	.010
	496	55	.010
	461	79	.010
	426	106	.010
	391	114	.010
	356	118	.020
	321	134	.030
	286	150	.020
	351	150	.020
North Charleston	11	42	.001
	15	71	.010
	23	48	.002
West Ashley	216	75	.002
	181	42	.001
	146	48	.001
	111	48	.001
	76	78	.002
	41	66	.001
	6	85	.003
Southern Rural County	55	Negligible	Negligible
	47	"	"
	35	"	"
	9	"	"
	7	"	"
	3	"	"
	37	"	"
	51	"	"
	67	"	"
Mount Pleasant	39	46	.002
	63	46	.001
	53	31	.001
Northern Rural County	43	Negligible	Negligible
	27	"	"
	31	"	"

[a]Interpolated from "Selected Suspended Particle Data," mimeographed, S.C. State Board of Health, Columbia.

[b]John C. Purvis, Alex J. Kish, and Norton D. Stromman, Air Pollution Diffusion Patterns for Use In Agricultural Planning in South Carolina, U.S. Department of Commerce in cooperation with South Carolina Agricultural Experiment Station, Clemson University, Clemson, South Carolina, Agricultural Weather Research Series No. 9, February, 1966, p. 18.

purposes of testing the hypothesis about the effect of air quality in the zone of residence on willingness to pay for air quality, it was decided to designate all zones where either particulate or sulfur dioxide concentrations exceeded a level that might threaten health as "dirty" zones. All others were designated as "clean" zones. Thus, zones where either estimated particulate concentration exceed $80 \mu g/m^3$ or sulfur dioxide concentration exceed 0.04 ppm were designated as dirty zones. Sulfur dioxide levels in some parts of Charleston County, too, on occasion, exceed the 0.04 ppm level, but no zones appeared in the sample where concentrations reached such a level. Consequently, the effective factor in determining classification of the zone of residence was particulate concentration. By the particulate criterion, seven of the thirty-four zones chosen for the sample were classified as dirty air zones.

EMPIRICAL ANALYSIS OF WILLINGNESS TO PAY FOR AIR QUALITY

Since data limitations were not as severe in testing hypotheses about willingness to pay for air quality as for water, the linear model of the analysis of variance problem for air quality includes all the hypothesized sources of variation; specifically, the model was of the form:

$$(Y_{ijk} - \overline{Y}) = b_1 Q_1 = b_2 Q_2 + \ldots + b_4 Q_4 + b_5 I_1 + b_6 I_2 + \ldots$$

$$b_{13} I_8 + b_{14} Z_1 + b_{15} Z_2 + b_{16} I_1 Z_1 + b_{17} I_1 Z_2 + \ldots b_{32} I_8 Z_2 +$$

$$e_{ijk}$$

where

Y_{ijk} = observed willingness to pay for the jth level of air quality by a household of the ith income level in a zone of air quality k;

$\overline{Y}$ = the mean willingness to pay for air quality at all levels by all households;

$b_1, b_2 \ldots b_{32}$ = coefficients on the deviation from the mean estimated by least-square;

$Q_1, Q_2 \ldots Q_4$ = zero-one variables indicating quality level (one for quality level j; zero for all others);

$I_1, I_2 \ldots I_8$ = zero-one variables indicating income level (one for income level i; zero for all others);

Z_1, Z_2 = zero-one variables indicating clean or dirty zone (one for zone k; zero otherwise);

$I_1 Z_1, I_1 Z_2 \ldots I_8 Z_2$ = zero-one variable indicating interaction (one for proper level, zero for all others);

e_{ijk} = error term associated with the Y_{ijk} observation.

A summary of analysis of variance in willingness to pay for air quality is presented in Table 13. The column labeled "Sum of Squares" shows the reduction in total sum of the squared deviations from the mean which are attributable to the hypothesized sources of variation. The mean square represents the average reduction of any particular quality level, income level, etc. The procedure is to evaluate this mean square relative to the error mean square to determine if it is significantly larger than can reasonably be expected due to chance. The calculated F is the ratio of the mean square for any source of variation to the error mean square. The probability of a calculated F being greater than any particular level has been worked out, and, as a result, one can test to see the probability of getting any particular calculated F simply by chance.

In Table 13 only one calculated F is statistically significant at the $\alpha = 0.10$ level, i.e., so large that only one time in nine it might not occur by chance. Variation in willingness to pay attributable to the quality levels of air quality is so great that there is only one chance in one hundred that it could be due to random chance. None of the other hypothesized sources of variation produce a large enough decrease in the squared deviations that they can be ruled significantly different from zero, however. Repeated computer runs and re-examination of the program for error did not produce any reduction at all (at the level of four digits to the right of the decimal) in the sum of

TABLE 13

Summary of Analysis of Variance in Willingness to Pay for
Air Quality, Charleston Metropolitan Area, 1968

Source of Variation	DF	Sum of Squares	Mean Square	Calculated F
Quality Levels	3	21.6047	7.2016	22.69*
Income Levels	7	0.9896	0.1414	0.45
Residence Zone	1	0.0000	—	—
Income-Zone Interaction	7	0.9532	0.1362	0.43
Error	821	260.5806	0.3174	
Total	829	284.2281		

*Significant at α 0.01 level.

Source: Calculated from household survey, Charleston Metropolitan Area, 1969.

squares attributable to the zone of residence.* We can conclude,
therefore, that quality levels do affect willingness to pay for air
quality—that is, we can reject null Hypothesis II ($\rho = 0$, all 1) and conclude that the effect of quality levels (at least some of them) on willingness to pay for air quality is greater than zero. Moreover, we can be
99 percent confident of our rejection of this null hypothesis. We do
not have sufficient evidence to reject any of the other null hypotheses
with regard to willingness to pay for air quality, however, (Failure
to reject a null hypothesis does not imply that it is true; it merely
means that the evidence at hand does not suggest it is not true.)

Estimates have also been made of the coefficients of the linear
model of variation around the mean willingness to pay for air quality.
The model, with coefficients, is

$$\hat{Y}_{ijk} - 1.675 = 2.761Q_1 - 1.124Q_2 - 0.990Q_3 - 0.648Q_4 - 0.278I_1 -$$
$$0.928I_2 + 0.022I_3 + 0.217I_4 + 1.145I_5 + 1.252I_6 - 0.242I_7 -$$
$$1.189I_8 - 0.444Z_1 + 0.444Z_2 - 0.283I_1Z_1 + 0.283I_1Z_2 +$$
$$0.661I_2Z_1 - 0.661I_2Z_2 + 0.618I_3Z_1 - 0.618I_3Z_2 - 0.542I_4Z_1$$
$$0.542I_4Z_2 + 0.088I_5Z_1 - 0.088I_5Z_2 + 0.054I_6Z_1 - 0.054I_6Z_2 +$$
$$0.425I_7Z_1 - 0.425I_7Z_2 - 1.021I_8Z_1 + 1.021I_8Z_2.$$

Special care should be exercised in interpreting these coefficients.
Firstly, only the first three coefficients (for Q_1, Q_2, and Q_3) are
significantly different from zero at the 95 percent level of confidence—
that is, random chance would have produced coefficients as large as
many of these 5 percent or more of the time. Since the other coefficients are not significantly different from zero, we cannot be sure
the signs represent the direction of the effect (if any) the variable
may have on variation around the mean willingness to pay for air
quality. Secondly, the coefficients are on variation around a mean
and not on variations around zero. Finally, all variables are discrete
terms; they are either zero or one, depending on the quality level

---

*The fact that the very dirty air zones at Charleston were not
selected by the random process for household sampling may partially
explain the lack of statistical significance of residence zone in affect-
ing willingness to pay. In none of the sampled zones was air quality
sufficiently low to cause persistent odor or hazing.

under consideration, the income level of the household, and the quality
of air in the zone of residence of that household.

EMPIRICAL ANALYSIS OF WILLINGNESS
TO PAY FOR WATER QUALITY

As we noted earlier, it was not possible to obtain data on water
quality in the individual residence zone of the Charleston area. Consequently, the linear model of the analysis of variance of willingness
to pay for water quality is much simpler than that for air quality:

$$(Y_{ijk} - \overline{Y}) = b_1 Q_1 + b_2 Q_2 + \ldots + b_4 Q_4 + b_5 I_1 + b_6 I_2 + \ldots +$$

$$b_{13} I_8 + e_{ijk}$$

where all terms are similar to those previously defined in the air
model.

A summary of the analysis of variance in willingness to pay for
water quality is presented in Table 14. The information in this table
is analogous to that in Table 13, except that there are only two
hypothesized sources of variation—quality levels and income levels.
Again, the calculated F ratio for reduction due to quality levels is
highly significant. There is less than one chance in 100 that the
reduction in variation due to quality levels which we have noted would
have occurred by random chance. Hence, we can again conclude that
quality levels do have an influence on the willingness of households
to pay for water quality. But, again, we have no evidence for a similar
conclusion relative to income levels. The reduction in the squared
deviations from the mean due to income levels is so small that we
cannot conclude it was not due to chance.

Estimates of the coefficients on the linear model for analysis
of variance in willingness to pay for water quality were also obtained.
They should be interpreted with the same caution noted with regard
to the air model. The model is:

$$\hat{Y}_{jik} - 1.844 = 3.063Q_1 - 1.097Q_2 - 0.934Q_3 - 1.032Q_4 -$$
$$0.138I_1 - 0.8541I_2 + 1.007I_3 - 0.365I_4 + 0.447I_5 + 1.032I_6 -$$
$$0.595I_7 - 0.533I_8.$$

All of the coefficients associated with quality levels in this model are
significantly different from zero at the 95 percent level of confidence.
None of the income coefficients are significant.

TABLE 14

Summary Analysis of Variance in Willingness to Pay for
Water Quality, Charleston Metropolitan Area, 1968

Source of Variation	DF	Sum of Squares	Mean Square	Calculated F
Quality Levels	3	26.3033	8.7678	21.19*
Income Levels	7	4.2415	0.6059	1.46
Error	829	343.0457	0.4138	
Total	839	373.5905		

*Significant at α 0.01 level.

Source: Calculated from household survey, Charleston Metropolitan Area, 1969.

SUMMARY OF STATISTICAL TESTING
OF HYPOTHESES

The two analyses of variance performed above produced almost identical results with regards to the hypotheses which were formulated. In both cases, we rejected the null format of Hypothesis II that the effect of quality level on willingness to pay for air or water quality was zero and concluded (with only one percent chance of error) that quality levels did, indeed, affect willingness to pay for both environmental goods. We were not able to reject the null format of any of the other hypotheses, however. Although the a priori logic still holds, we do not yet have ample evidence to reject the null hypotheses:

Hypothesis I: $\alpha_j = 0$, all j

Hypothesis III: $\delta_k = 0$, all k

Hypothesis IV: $(\alpha\delta)_{jk} = 0$, all j, all k

The size of the sample may be responsible for our failure to reject at least some of these hypotheses. Later, we will analyze the sample size and see that some income classes were seriously undersampled. Thus, given the variance in the population, our sample may not have been powerful enough to detect effects on willingness to pay which can be detected with a larger sample. At this point, however, we have no evidence to support the notion that income levels or environmental quality in the zone of residence affect the percent of their income which people are willing to pay for environmental goods.

OBSERVATIONS ON THE AGGREGATES

Given the lack of statistical significance in the estimate of the percentage of gross annual income which households of varying income classes are willing to pay for clean air and clean water, it is probably not legitimate to expand the sample data to the total population by income classes. Nevertheless, the sample data are statistically significant with regards to variation in willingness to pay due to quality levels, and, since this is a pilot study, it may be interesting to examine the total dollars which residents of the Charleston area might be willing to devote annyally to obtaining various levels of air and/or water quality.

Aggregate sums on the dollars Charleston area households are willing to pay for four levels of air quality are shown in Table 15.

TABLE 15

Willingness to Pay in Aggregate Sums for Four Alternative Levels of Air Quality by
Household Income Class, Charleston Metropolitan Area, 1968

| Household | | Amount To: | | |
Income Class	Avoid Perceptible Odor	Avoid Haze or Smog	Avoid Soiling of Materials	Ensure No Threat to Health
Under $3,000	$ 152,901	$ 77,591	$ 86,720	$ 712,015
3,000-5,999	799,083	370,102	428,981	2,388,838
6,000-8,999	1,678,570	1,219,474	774,726	8,765,864
9,000-11,999	2,060,736	1,613,445	654,963	4,233,296
12,000-14,999	762,986	586,913	586,913	8,803,688
15,000-17,999	1,937,364	1,788,336	1,508,908	5,514,036
18,000-20,999	427,272	427,272	427,272	3,221,498
Over $21,000	—	—	—	2,330,580
Total*	$7,818,912	$6,083,133	$4,468,483	$35,969,715

*Significantly different from zero and each other at the α 0.01 level.

Source: Calculated from sample survey of households.

123

All totals are significantly different from zero and from each other at the α 0.01 level. Attention should be focused primarily on the totals for each column. The columns are arranged, left to right, in ascending order by engineering or technical standards—that is, technically speaking, "no threat to health" represents the highest quality level and "no perceptible odor" represents the lowest. The respondent households indicated a different ordering, however, with regards to willingness to pay. "No threat to health" was considered the most valuable quality level, and, for it, the households of the Charleston metropolitan area indicated a willingness to pay nearly $36 million in total. The next most important quality level, however, in terms of willingness to pay, was "no perceptible odor" (the lowest level by technical standards). Reading across the totals row in Table 15, from left to right, we see that households are apparently not willing to pay more to obtain quality levels high enough to ensure no smog or no soiling than they are willing to pay to avoid odors in the air. The conclusion is that households will not pay to avoid smog or soiling unless, in the bargain, they get air quality high enough that it assures no threat to health or unless they can obtain air with no perceptible odor at a cost considerably below the maximum amount they would be willing to pay for it.

Willingness to pay, in aggregate sums, for four levels of water quality can be seen in Table 16. Here, too, all totals are significantly different from zero at the α 0.01 level (that is, there is only one chance in 100 that we would obtain totals as high as those shown if the true willingness to pay were zero). As we noted earlier, the technical ordering on these water quality levels is somewhat more ambiguous than that on the four levels of air quality, yet the ordering in Table 16, from left to right, probably represents increasing technical standards. Unlike the results on air quality, however, the ordering on willingness to pay does not differ in any meaningful way from the technical ordering. While the absolute aggregate willingness to pay for water clean enough to swim in safely is slightly lower than that for water clean enough to fish in safely, our sampling error is large enough to prevent us from concluding that aggregate willingness to pay for these two levels of water quality is, in fact, different.* We can conclude with a high degree of confidence that willingness to pay for water clean enough to fish is safely is greater than willingness to pay for

---

*There is better than a fifty-fifty chance that the difference noted in Table 16 between aggregate willingness to pay for water clean enough to fish in safely and water clean enough to swim in safely in due to sampling error.

TABLE 16

Willingness to Pay in Aggregate Sums for Four Alternative
Levels of Water Quality by Household Income Class,
Charleston Metropolitan Area, 1968

Household Income Class	Avoid Unpleasant Smell	Clean Enough to Fish Safely	Clean Enough to Swim Safely	Safe Drinking Water
Under $3,000	$ 176,700	$ 294,065	$ 118,017	$ 811,449
3,000-5,999	254,302	606,403	254,302	2,053,946
6,000-8,999	1,090,353	1,061,659	1,362,941	12,596,447
9,000-11,999	1,063,318	1,421,748	1,693,318	4,584,739
12,000-14,999	845,154	962,537	903,845	8,392,849
15,000-17,999	1,611,365	1,723,136	1,900,107	5,374,322
18,000-20,999	250,938	427,272	257,719	2,373,735
Over $21,000	—	—	—	2,223,165
Total	$5,922,130[a]	$6,496,820[b]	$6,490,249[b]	$38,410,652[a]

[a]Significantly different from zero and other levels at α 0.01 level.
[b]Significantly different from zero, but not significantly different from each other at α 0.01 level.

Source: Calculated from sample survey of households.

125

water which has no odor, and that willingness to pay for "safe drinking water" is greater than that for any of the other three levels of quality.

The "safe drinking water" sum in Table 16 requires some further explanation. It seems reasonable to conclude that most respondents interpreted the question pertaining to this quality level in a fairly broad sense—that is, their answer, in terms of willingness to pay, was based on the thought that they were hypothetically purchasing an assured adequate and safe supply of drinking water. The $38.4 million figure, therefore, represents not only the willingness to pay for pristine clean water in every stream, water clean enough to drink without treatment, but willingness to pay for enough water that can be treated to the point that it will safely assure the area of an adequate supply for drinking purposes. Interpreted in this fashion, the $38.4 million per year does not seem an unduly large amount.

EVALUATION OF THE PILOT SURVEY

The optimum size of a sample is dependent not upon the size of the population being sampled, but upon the variance in that population and the degree of accuracy required. The data obtained from the pilot survey of willingness to pay for clean air and clean water in the Charleston metropolitan area provide an objective basis for estimating the true variance of the population and, thus, for judging the size of the sample required to obtain more accurate estimates of the true willingness to pay for these environmental goods. Using variances for each income class, pooled across quality levels, we can employ Stein's two-stage sampling procedure to calculate the sample sizes required to obtain estimates of willingness to pay at different levels of precision.[3]

Table 17 shows the sample sizes required in order to be able to estimate the true willingness to pay for air quality with 95 percent confidence where we desire estimates that are within a range of, plus or minus, one percentage point, one-half a percentage point, or one-tenth a percentage point of the true percentage of gross annual income the households are willing to pay. The pilot sample size appears to be adequate for estimates within the one percentage point range in the two lower income classes.

The variance on the mean willingness to pay for these two income classes was relatively small. There are very high variances, however, on two income classes—the $6,000-8,999 class and the $12,000-14,999 class. In these latter classes, the pilot survey seriously undersampled.

TABLE 17

Comparison of Pilot Sample Size and Estimates of Required Sample Sizes
for Alternative Confidence Intervals on Percentage of Gross Income Willing
to Be Paid for Air Quality, Charleston Metropolitan Area, 1968

Income Class	Pilot Sample Size	Pooled Variance (all quality levels)	Estimated Sample Size Required for 95 Percent Confidence Interval in Percentage Points:			
			± 1.0	± 0.5	± 0.1
Under $3,000	35	6.15	26	104	260
3,000–5,999	43	2.85	14	56	140
6,000–8,999	44	62.19	253	912	2,530
9,000–11,999	35	15.19	63	252	630
12,000–14,999	20	128.76	560	2,244	5,600
15,000–17,999	13	15.93	74	296	740
18,000–20,999	8	3.37	15	60	150
Over $21,000	3	*	–	–	–
Total	201		1,005	3,924	10,050

*Pilot sample too small for valid estimate.

Source: Calculated using Stein's two-stage sampling procedure (see Steel and Torrie, pp. 86–67).

Moreover, the pilot survey seriously undersampled in the highest income class, where only three households were surveyed. All in all,
it appears that a sample of at least 1,000 households is required if one
is to obtain estimates of the true willingness to pay that one can be
highly confident of falling within a range of plus or minus one percentage point. Closer ranges of accuracy require sample sizes that increase with the reciprocal of the square of the confidence interval.

Table 18 is similar to Table 17. It shows sample size required
to obtain estimates of willingness to pay for water quality. Again, the
size of the pilot survey appears adequate for the two lowest-income
classes. But, again, we see that the variance on willingness to pay is
high for households in the income classes of $6,000-8,999 and $12,000-
14,999. A sample that allowed 95 percent confidence on estimates
of willingness to pay within a range of plus or minus one percentage
point would need to be larger for water quality than that for air quality
by a total of 167 households. Since estimates on willingness to pay
for both air and water quality were obtained on the sample, it appears
that a sample of approximately 1,200 households was needed and would
be called for in any future effort.

STRATIFIED SAMPLING VERSUS COMPLETELY
RANDOM SAMPLING

The estimates of the optimum-size sample made above are
based on the assumption of a stratified sample. The relatively high
variances in some income classes suggest that these classes needed
to be sampled in much higher proportion than their occurrence in the
population. One can obtain the accuracy needed on these income
classes only if he increases the size of the total sample to the level
that large numbers of households in these income classes are included
strictly by completely random selection or if he stratifies the sample
and randomly selects within the various income classes based on the
variance of the income class. The latter alternative is less costly.

There are some practical problems connected with drawing a
stratified sample based on income classes, however. Usually one
does not have a priori information in great detail on the spatial distribution of household income within a region. It is possible to
identify some areas as high-income zones and others as low-income
zones, but this identification is seldom precise. Any land area used
as a sampling unit is likely to have a mixture of household income
levels. Consequently, one cannot control completely the number of
households of any income class which will appear in the sample. The

TABLE 18

Comparison of Pilot Sample Size and Estimates of Required Sample Sizes
for Alternative Confidence Intervals on Percentage of Gross Income Willing
to Be Paid for Water Quality, Charleston Metropolitan Area, 1968

Income Class	Pilot Sample Size	Pooled Variance (all quality levels)	Estimated Sample Size Required for 95 Percent Confidence Interval in Percentage Points:		
			± 1.0	± 0.5	± 0.1
Under $3,000	35	8.58	35	140	350
3,000–5,999	43	3.43	14	56	140
6,000–8,999	44	108.51	436	1,744	4,360
9,000–11,999	35	12.75	53	212	530
12,000–14,999	20	127.21	554	2,216	4,540
15,000–17,999	13	13.66	64	256	640
18,000–20,999	8	3.74	16	54	160
Over $21,000	3	*	–	–	–
Total	201		1,172	4,578	11,720

*Pilot sample too small for valid estimate.

Source: Calculated using Stein's two-stage sampling procedure (see Steel and Torrie, pp. 86–87).

result is that, even with a stratified sample, some oversampling (above the optimum) will probably be necessary.

THE VALUE OF CONJECTURAL ESTIMATES

Earlier, we noted that one cannot be sure that respondents in a survey will interpret questions in the way the researcher intended or that the respondent will behave in a real situation as he indicated he would behave in the hypothetical situation. The answers received to questions in this pilot survey were strictly conjectural, and one must be somewhat cautious in placing great significance on their magnitude. Yet the results of the pilot survey show figures for willingness to pay which are significantly different from zero at a high level of statistical confidence. Our sample was too small to provide precise estimates on aggregate willingness to pay, but the estimates which were obtained appear to be reasonable in view of the overall household income of the Charleston area. Where the willingness to pay estimates are rather high, as in the case of "no threat to health" from air pollution and safe drinking water, they can be rationalized. Likewise, variations in the ordering on willingness to pay can also be rationalized. That does not mean that the rationalizations are correct, but it does suggest that a survey of the general type used in this pilot effort can obtain useful results.

NOTES

1. Ronald G. Ridker, Economic Costs of Air Pollution: Studies in Measurement (New York: Praeger, 1967), p. 19.

2. John C. Purvis, Alex J. Kish, and Norton D. Stromman, Air Pollution Diffusion Patterns for Use in Agricultural Planning in South Carolina, U.S. Department of Commerce in cooperation with South Carolina Agricultural Experiment Station, Clemson University, Clemson, S. C., Agricultural Weather Research Series No. 9, February, 1966, p. 18.

3. Robert G.D. Steel and James H. Torrie, Principles and Procedures of Statistics (New York: McGraw-Hill, 1960), pp. 86-7.

9

THE USE
OF ECONOMIC ANALYSIS
IN
ENVIRONMENTAL
PLANNING

We have contended throughout this book that economic logic and the analysis which stems from that logic can be used effectively in managing the resources of the coastal zone to ensure an adequate supply of environmental goods. Yet we must admit that even nonpecuniary economic analysis cannot answer all the questions that confront resource planners and managers. We have built models which are amenable to application of economic logic, but they are limited in their ability to solve many of the practical problems which demand solution. In this chapter, we will explore the meaning of economic analysis in environmental planning and point out some of the ways in which the analysis demonstrated in the previous chapters might be used by resource planners faced with the necessity of seeking economic-environmental balance, with special reference to the coastal zone.

MINIMUM-DAMAGE PLANNING

Earlier in this report, we defined economics as the science of values and choices. Implicit in that definition is the assumption that, give a set of values, individuals seek to make those choices which either maximize their satisfaction or minimize their losses. Consequently, much economic analysis is concerned with evaluating the costs associated with alternative courses of action in an effort to determine that course of action which will result in the least cost or the minimum damages. To the resource planner, such analysis can be especially useful since it can help him to chart a plan of resource uses which will meet the needs of society at the least possible cost.

Least-cost, or minimum-damage, models have been developed in many forms as part of the great body of work utilizing operations research and systems analysis. The Harvard Water Project expended considerable time and money in developing and adapting such models for use in water resources planning.[1] While formal least-cost models can be quite useful, they can also become enormously complicated. Even given the unlikely possibility that we can accumulate all the data needed to implement such a model and that we have adequate knowledge of the functional relationships which tie those data together,[2] we may still face problems of solving the model for an optimal solution. Say there are sixteen major industries which can be regulated at any of three possible output levels; we are faced with the problem of evaluating 3^{16} possible management schemes. This is too large a number of schemes for evaluation by even the fastest computer, and experience of highly competent researchers has indicated that formal optimalizing models may not be very helpful in obtaining solutions to the practical resource management problems of local and regional planning agencies.*

Professor John Kissin has noted some other limitations associated with the use of highly formal policy models for resource planning. These limitations arise out of three kinds of changes occurring over time: (1) changes in our knowledge about the world and the ecologic system; (2) changes in technology which drastically restructure our life-styles (sometimes over relatively short periods of time); and (3) changes in the values we place on environmental quality. As a result of these inevitable changes, Kissin believes long-range planning is a dubious undertaking. To Kissin, the hope of eliminating all future conflicts through use of highly sophisticated system models is "wholly illusory." Instead, he suggests we center our attention on planning activities which will not necessarily eliminate future resource management problems but simply make them less serious than the problems we currently face.[3]

While we may despair somewhat about the use of formal least-cost models, an economic evaluation of the costs of alternative courses of action in resources management is possible and practical. Many of the decisions relative to resources use in the coastal zone center on only a few alternative courses of action. For example, regional planners may face such questions as to whether the location of a new chemical plant on an estuary will be beneficial to the region or whether the development of a recreational complex will create enough income

---

*We are indebted to Clifford S. Russell of Resources for the Future, Inc. , for comments on these points.

to offset any environmental damages. Partial answers to these questions can be had if we can estimate the pecuniary effects of the proposed development and compare those effects to the environmental damages likely to result. Failure to acquire the chemical plant or the recreational complex will result in pecuniary damages to the region, and acquisition of these developments will result in environmental damages. Yet too often we have had only the haziest ideas about the relative magnitude of these damages. Economic evaluation can be a practical method of determining which course of action will result in the minimum damage.

SYNTHESIS FOR ECONOMIC EVALUATION

In the preceding chapters we have developed in parallel fashion two facets of the economic analysis needed to evaluate damages resulting from alternative resources uses in the coastal zone: (1) an economic-ecologic linkages model showing the environmental repercussions of alternative changes in economic activity and (2) willingness-to-pay estimates for various levels of environmental quality. The economic-ecologic linkages model allows us to quantify the environmental residuals associated with the generation of $1 of local pecuniary income and, conversely, the price, in terms of pecuniary income, which a region must pay to avoid increasing the residuals which it emits into the environment. The willingness-to-pay estimates can also be interpreted as household estimates of the damages resulting from deterioration of air and water quality below certain specified levels. Hence, the economic-ecologic linkages model provides us with estimates of the costs of refraining from pollution, and the willingness-to-pay estimates help us to assess the social costs that are likely to result if we do not refrain. Given this information, the solution appears simple and straightforward: We will choose that course of action which appears to have the least cost.

As we noted at the end of Chapter 4, however, such a straightforward solution may ignore some important considerations. For example, the damages resulting from pollution may be rather widespread, falling on all social classes and all neighborhoods, but the pecuniary income resulting from a new chemical plant or recreational complex may be limited to a relatively few workers and business people who serve those workers. At best, therefore, the simple solution outlined above can give us only aggregate minimum damages; it can tell us little about the distribution of damages resulting from the alternative courses of action. Moreover, the limits imposed by the built-in assumptions of the economic-ecologic linkages model and the conjectural nature of the willingness-to-pay estimates cannot be ignored in interpreting the results of such economic evaluation of damages. The assumption of constant technology, for example, results in the economic-ecologic linkages model producing residuals which may be tied to production processes which will be radically altered in any new plant. Finally, the aggregation problem alluded to in Chapter 7 severely limits the usefulness of the model in estimating the environmental residuals associated with specific new plants. Consequently, our evaluation of alternative damages must be viewed as highly aggregated estimates, or first approximations, of the actual damages. Nevertheless, first approximations of possible damages may be quite useful (especially when planning must otherwise be based on guesses and intuition), if the planner is careful to recognize that such estimates are not definitive.

AN APPLICATION FOR THE CHARLESTON AREA

We noted in Chapter 5 that the Charleston area represents a case where the conflicts between economic growth and the maintenance of environmental quality in the coastal zone can be readily observed. We have used the Charleston area as a case study for the empirical implementation of the economic analysis developed in the previous chapters. Now we may ask in a very specific way how our study can be used by Charleston area planners to evaluate alternatives for the future development of that area.

The Office of Business Economics (OBE), U.S. Department of Commerce, has prepared a consistent set of national-regional forecasts of population, employment, output-per-worker, and income data for the United States and for a national grid of economic sub-areas, one of which is centered on Charleston. Forecasts are made for 1970, 1980, etc., forward to the year 2020. Although there is no assurance that the Charleston area will grow as the OBE forecasts indicate, these forecasts can be used for demonstration purposes to show how a planner might evaluate the possible environmental damages associated with economic development in the area and the possible pecuniary damages associated with failure to achieve such economic growth.

In order to use the OBE projections for demonstration purposes, we must make some assumptions required by the nature of the basic input-output data: (1) we must assume that the technology of production in the Charleston area in 1980 will be the same as in the present (an admittedly unrealistic assumption); (2) we must assume that the proportion of total output of basic industries sold to external buyers remains constant from the present to 1980; and (3) the value which residents of the area place on various levels of environmental quality will also remain constant. The delineation of the Charleston subarea by OBE does not coincide exactly with the three-county study area, so we must also adjust our data to remove Colleton County.

Table 19 presents projected increases in pecuniary income in the 1968-80 period in the Charleston area resulting from the growth of five selected basic industries. The income multipliers obtained from mutliplying value-added coefficients by each element in the Leontief inverse of the input-output matrix indicate that growth in output of these five industries will account for a growth in annual local pecuniary income of $74,049,000 by 1980. The environmental price which Charleston area residents will be forced to pay for this pecuniary income, however (assuming constant technology), includes a 23.40 percent increase in the level of particulate concentration in the atmosphere and a 44.13 percent increase in concentration of sulfur dioxide. Although the particulate levels in many parts of the Charleston area are already above the level which is considered safe for health, these increases in air pollution will result in an increase in the extent of the area which suffers from pollution levels sufficiently high to threaten the health of human beings. The increase in sulfur dioxide levels are of special interest, since, in 1968, there were relatively few zones in the Charleston area where concentration was high enough to threaten health, but, by 1980, sulfur dioxide concentrations may begin to be a health hazard in much of the Charleston area (see Table 12). The concentration level of SO_2 which is generally considered to pose a threat to health is 0.04 ppm or more.

Examination of the environmental repercussions of the projected growth of individual industries provides some insight into the possible trade-offs between regional environmental quality and increases in pecuniary income. The textile and apparel industry, for example is expected to account for more than 70 percent of the increase of income in 1980 over 1968 levels. Yet the environmental repercussions of growth in textiles and apparel are relatively minor, accounting for less than 2 percent of the increase in residuals emitted into the environment. In contrast, chemical manufacturing is expected to increase 1980 Charleston area income over 1968 levels by about $9,562,000 (about 13 percent of the total increase), while increasing the sulfur dioxide in the atmosphere by more than 40 percent. That is, 13 percent of the projected income increase accounts for more than 92 percent of the expected increase in atmospheric sulfur dioxide.

TABLE 19

Projected Increases in Income and Total Emissions of Selected Industrial
Sectors, Charleston Metropolitan Area, 1968–80

Industrial Sectors	Projected 1968–80 Income Increases[a] (in thousands)	Projected 1968–80 Increases in Total Emissions of:[b]	
		Particulates (in percent)	Sulfur Dioxide (in percent)
Food & Kindred Products	3	c	c
Textile & Apparel	53,477	.38	1.77
Lumber, Pulp, & Paper	5,353	5.15	.67
Chemical Manufacturing	9,562	.08	40.45
Petroleum & Coal Products	5,654	17.79	1.24
Total Selected Sectors	74,049	23.40	44.13

[a]Based on adjusted unpublished OBE forecasts of Charleston area economic activity for 1980.
[b]Calculated using the economic-ecologic linkages model in Chapter 7.
[c]The quantity of direct and indirect emissions is less than .0001 units.

Since the above analysis reveals that the growth of the chemical industry in the Charleston area may result in increases in the level of sulfur dioxide in the atmosphere to the point of threatening the health of some of the residents, we can use our estimates of willingness to pay to avoid air pollution that threatens health and obtain a measure of environmental damages resulting from growth of the chemical industry. In Chapter 8, we determined that Charleston area residents were willing to sacrifice up to $35,969,715 a year to prevent air quality from causing a threat to health. The growth of the chemical industry will add only $9,562,000 annually to the income of Charleston area residents. Consequently, we may conclude that, unless the chemical industry can alter its production technology to drastically reduce its emissions of sulfur dioxide, the Charleston area will suffer less aggregate damage from restricting the growth of chemical manufacturing than it will if the chemical industry is allowed to grow at projected levels. Similar analysis reveals that projected growth of the lumber, pulp, and paper industry will result in increases in the level of particulates so that the environmental damage is greater than the pecuniary opportunity foregone.

THE STATE OF THE ART

As we have seen in this chapter, the techniques of economic analysis presented in this report are not definitive. There are many technical problems which still remain if an economic analysis is to be applied to environmental problems in a comprehensive way. We have attempted to present a framework for such a comprehensive approach and to point out areas where additional thought and research is needed to make such an approach practical and useful to those charged with responsibility for managing the natural resources of the coastal zone.

Further research on a multidisciplinary front is badly needed. We must continue to develop and refine such general equilibrium concepts as those suggested by Ayres and Kneese[4] and the model presented in this report. We must have additional quantitative information about the relationships of various outputs into the environment and the ability of that environment to support a healthy and satisfying life. Economists are not qualified to gather and evaluate these data, and research on a broad, multidisciplinary front will be necessary if the proper understanding is to be achieved.[5] We must think systematically about who receives the benefits of pollutant control and who pays for the control and incorporate the results of such thinking into our analysis. Research in all these areas is now under way, but it is often being done on an isolated, narrow basis, and its practical usefulness as an input into a systems-type approach to environmental planning is limited to the fact that it was not conceived as part of the whole. Economics is a coordinating discipline, and economic analysis, such as that presented in this volume, can be useful (if in no other way) in defining the data needs and stimulating the necessary research.

We have only begun to explore the analytical possibilities of the analytical devices presented in this report. They appear to be highly flexible devices when the proper data can be obtained. For example, data can be substituted into the overall framework at will and the effect noted, and it is possible to update our analysis as technology changes. But they are still crude devices, and they cannot be used as strictly a mechanical substitute for human judgment. The final decisions about our environment will be made by men.

NOTES

1. Arthur Maass, ed., Design of Water Resource Systems: New Techniques for Relating Economic Objectives, Engineering Analysis, and Government Planning (Cambridge, Mass.: Harvard University Press, 1962).

2. For a review of some of the problems associated with the use of formal models for coastal zone resource management and policy, see Maynard M. Hufschmidt, Hugh Knox, and Francis Parker, "A Policy Analysis Approach to Coastal Zone Management: Objectives, Alternative Development Strategies and Econometric Models," in James C. Hite and James M. Stepp, ed., Coastal Zone Resource Management (New York: Praeger, 1971), pp. 104-20.

3. John Kissin, "Flexibility and Data Needs in Coastal Zone Planning", in Hite and Stepp, pp. 121-26.

4. Robert V. Ayres and Allen V. Kneese, "Production, Consumption and Externalities," American Economic Review, LIX, 284-85.

5. See Kissin on this point.

10

In the previous chapter, we discussed possible application of the economic analysis developed in this report to problems of evaluating planning alternatives for resource use in the coastal zone. In this chapter we will explore some types of institutions which might be needed to make use of such planning techniques. In doing so, we realize that these techniques are far from definitive. Our attention will focus on such questions as: (1) what types of organizational arrangements will be needed to use the procedures developed in this report; (2) what types of personnel will be needed to staff these planning organizations; (3) how can we economize in obtaining the requisite data and in making the necessary calculations; and (4) what will be the administrative cost of implementing the procedures which we have suggested? Finally, we will develop a scenario to illustrate how all these institutional arrangements might be meshed to help answer the planning problems which have arisen in the coastal zone.

ORGANIZING FOR THE PLANNING JOB

Although all citizens of the United States have a vital interest in rational management of coastal zone resources, and, consequently, all levels of government have legitimate concern in the evaluation of alternative uses of these resources, there are persuasive arguments for concluding that the primary responsibility for coastal zone planning and management rests at the state level. The federal government is too remote to fully appreciate all the regional idiosyncrasies and needs which should be considered in developing a balanced management plan. The use of regional environmental-ecologic linkage models in this report rests on the assumption that such considerations as

141

local income and development needs must be given particular attention.
Very small, local areas, however, may be too small to maintain viable
planning agencies. Moreover, such local areas may be subject to
strong temptations to sacrifice environmental quality for a new industrial plant that will produce tangible income in the form of dollars.
For all these reasons, therefore, we will assume that the primary
responsiblity for the public management of coastal resources lies at
the state level.[1]

In most coastal states, there are many state agencies which
have traditional and/or legal interests in the management of the coastal
zone. In Chapter 1 we noted that at least a part of the coastal zone
management problem arises out of the interagency conflicts over
jurisdiction. Consequently, one of the first institutional tasks requisite to rational management of coastal resources is determination
of just who is to call the shots. It may be neither necessary nor
desirable, however, for all power relative to coastal zone management to be vested in one state agency. What is needed is the desig-
nation of one state agency as the "lead agency," with authority to
coordinate a coastal zone management program. In most states, a
smoothly functioning management system will require that all agencies
with a legitimate concern with coastal resources be included in management planning and operations.

One possible institutional arrangement for accommodating this
need might be a Coastal Zone Management Council, composed of
representatives of such state agencies as the Pollution Control Authority, the Fish and Wildlife Commission, the Tourist and Recreation
agency, and the Division of Industrial Development. The traditions
and governmental structure of each state will dictate just which
agencies should be represented on the council, and while there may
be definite administrative efficiencies associated with keeping the
size of the council rather small, the realities of bureaucratic life
dictate that no relevant agency be excluded.

The Coastal Zone Management Council might function much
like the planning commission of units of local government. All rec-
ommendations for coastal zone management should be approved by
this council before either direct action is taken or legislation is in-
itiated. In most states, the council's principal activity would be
focused on the review of applications for permits for various types
of development in the coastal zone. Given the proper procedures to
insure constitutional guarantees of due process, the council might be
empowered to issue or deny permits for withdrawal of water and/or
for the discharge of waste in the coastal zone. The council may also

be authorized to speak for the state government on permit applications to such federal agencies as the Army Corps of Engineers. Regardless of the scope of the council's authority, however, no coastal zone management plan is likely to be effective without broad public support, and the Coastal Zone Management Council should be empowered—even required—to hold public hearings on all matters of more than routine importance.

Any scientific approach to coastal zone management will require that a trained, professional planning staff be assembled to provide technical services to the policy body. Ideally, such a staff should consist of at least one land-use planner, an economist-statistician, an ecologist, and an environmental systems engineer, plus several subprofessional clerks and assistants. All of the professional staff should possess advanced degrees or comparable experience in their field. In practice, however, a coastal zone planning staff may be assembled initially using some part-time professional services, either borrowed from other state agencies or contracted from consultants. Yet, use of the planning tools developed in this study will require that at least one or two highly qualified planner-economists be employed on a full-time basis to supervise assembly of the needed planning tools and to ensure their proper use.

Finally, if we are to adequately plan for the use of coastal resources and translate those plans into an operative management program, provision must be made to enforce the management plan. Enforcement will almost certainly be difficult. It will require constant surveillance in order to stop violations before irreversible damage is done. In many states, the conservation officers of the Fish and Wildlife Commission may be in a good position to assume a large measure of the enforcement responsibility. But development of a coastal zone management organization, regardless of the level of sophistication of its planning and action, will require that adequate funding be made available to enforce the management plan.

ASSEMBLING THE PLANNING TOOLS

Regardless of the organizational structure established for the management of the coastal zone, rational management requires adequate planning tools. One of the chief purposes of this volume was the development of some of these tools. The planning techniques discussed in previous chapters center on three essential elements: (1) an input-output model of a local or regional economy; (2) an environmental matrix showing the inputs and outputs into the environment of each sector of the economy; and (3) some estimates of the willingness of residents to sacrifice income in order to preserve or restore certain levels of environmental quality. We have used the Charleston area as a case study to illustrate the problems associated with empirically developing these tools, and we can only conclude that these problems are substantial but not insurmountable. The question may be asked, however, whether it is practical for a state coastal zone management agency to attempt to assemble and use these tools.

The construction of a relevant input-output model is likely to pose the most serious problem to a state coastal zone management agency wishing to use the planning techniques developed in this study. An environmental matrix can be constructed largely from secondary sources since it is not likely to require extensive modification to fit regional circumstances. One national environmental matrix, constructed at a relatively disaggregated level for the industrial sectors, could be easily modified to fit the industrial mix of the local or state economy. The willingness to pay for environmental quality may be obtained either from a study of land values in areas of various levels of pollution, as suggested by Nourse and Crocker, [2] or from a household survey such as the one used in the Charleston study. Neither method is likely to yield highly precise estimates, but either method will probably produce usable results. And the cost of either a property-values study or a small household survey is likely to be relatively low. Furthermore, once the willingness-to-pay estimates are obtained, they may be used for two or three years before they will need to be updated. While the input-output model may also be used for several years (perhaps for as many as five years), a unique matrix must be constructed for every locality or region. The cost of constructing such a matrix from survey data is enormous—$100,000 or more. And the construction of an input-output matrix requires a highly skilled professional staff. Consequently, if the planning techniques developed in the previous chapters are to be of practical aid in the management of coastal resources, we must explore ways for economizing in the construction of the needed input-output matrixes.

There are at least two ways in which the costs of obtaining the needed input-output matrixes may be reduced: (1) simulate the regional input-output matrixes by adjusting the national input-output model, using one of the approaches discussed at the close of Chapter 6, and (2) construct a state input-output model from primary data and evaluate all planning alternatives within the context of the state economy. Of these two possibilities, the latter is probably the more practical for a state agency. Although considerable investment will be needed if the state model is to be constructed from primary data, the cost of constructing the model can be spread across many state agencies which can use the model in their work. For example, a state input-output model can be an extremely valuable tool in estimating state revenues and planning the state budget. It can also be useful to state industrial development agencies in analyzing market potential within the state for particular types of industries. Several states have already developed input-output models for their economies, and it is not unlikely that many other states will follow suit in the near future.* Moreover, state government often routinely collects a vast amount of statistical data, and these routine reports from business and industry in the state may need only slight alteration to allow the state agencies to construct an input-output model without the necessity of a separate survey.

At several earlier points in this volume, we have noted that the lower the level of industrial aggregation on the planning model, the greater the precision of estimates. If a state input-output model is to be used in coastal zone planning, the level of industrial aggregation becomes especially important. If, for example, the state input-output model aggregates all chemical manufacturing into one sector and we are concerned with analysis of the effects of a fertilizer plant on the coastal environment, the model may estimate environmental repercussions which will not, in fact, occur or fail to estimate such repercussions as will occur, simply because the model cannot distinguish between a fertilizer plant and all other types of chemical manufacturers. A state model, of necessity, will diffuse indirect effects of a particular change in economic activity throughout the entire state economy, and, if it is sensitive to only the grossest linkages between very broad industry groups, it may produce results which are essentially worthless. Construction of a state model at a low level of industrial aggregation will not eliminate diffusion of indirect effects throughout the state, but it will mean that the model will be more sensitive to actual interindustry linkages and, thus, more likely to yield useful results.

MAKING THE SYSTEM WORK

Although we have looked at the pieces of a coastal zone management system, we must still put these pieces together and establish

---

*Some of the states which currently have input-output models are California, Washington, Utah, Kansas, Oklahoma, and West Virginia.

procedures for their administration. Every state will need to establish procedures which fit its own particular needs, but much of the day-to-day activity of a state coastal zone management agency is likely to be focused on applications for permits to use and develop coastal resources. Administrative procedures must be established, therefore, to process these applications and to ensure that they are properly evaluated.

One possible procedure for processing permit applications is the system currently in use in South Carolina. With relatively simple modifications, this system could effectively use the planning tools which we have developed and illustrated in the previous chapters. Basically, the South Carolina procedure involves five steps:[3]

1. Notices of permit applications are submitted to the State Water Resources Commission and other relevant state agencies. The Water Resources Commission functions as the "lead" agency with regard to processing the applications and it is charged with responsibility for making a final recommendation concerning disposal of the application.*

2. At its discretion, the Water Resources Commission may require permit applicants to publish notice describing their application in a newspaper of general circulation in the county in which the development is proposed. The notice must run at least once in each of two consecutive weeks. Failure to make proof of such publication when requested results in automatic objection to the permit.

3. During the two weeks in which public notice is given of the permit application, appropriate state agencies are requested to submit written comments of the application. These comments, together with any comments elicited by the newspaper notices, become a part of the permanent file of the water Resources Commission.

4. If public response to the newspaper notices and/or the comments of state agencies indicate any appreciable objection to the permit, the Water Resources Commission may call a public hearing to review all aspects of the application. The commission may omit the public hearing, however, if there is no adverse comment.

---

*In South Carolina, the ultimate decision to approve or reject the permit application is made by the State Budget and Control Board.

5. After reviewing all comments, the Water Resources Commission prepares a report with a recommendation either for issuance or denial of the permit application. In its report, the commission reviews any adverse or conflicting comments and cites reasons for its recommendation.

While the South Carolina procedure outlined above has several limitations, it appears to offer the framework around which a workable coastal zone management system might be built. As it is presently constituted, the South Carolina system is an ad hoc process. The Water Resources Commission has only a small professional staff, and there is no one assigned to evaluate each application rigorously. Reliance is placed on the newspaper-reading public and each of the state agencies to raise pertinent objections to an application, Moreover, since South Carolina has no comprehensive coastal zone management plan, each permit application is examined on its own merits without reference to a long-range system of uses for the coastal resources. The addition of a professional planning staff such as suggested earlier in this chapter, however, would allow the South Carolina Water Resources Commission to develop such a comprehensive management plan and to scrutinize each permit application independently. It is likely that many other coastal states could also modify their existing administrative procedure to introduce comprehensive planning and evaluation with as much ease.

CLOSING REMARKS

At the close of the preceding chapter, we observed that no economic model—indeed, no model of any sort—can automatically solve the vast array of management problems in the coastal zone. These models must function within a framework of human institutions, and human institutions grow out of the traditions of our history and the bio-anthropological imperatives of the evolution of the human animal. No amount of technology—not even that required to transport man to the planets—can alter the basic fact of man's nature, and no institution can be successful if it fails to recognize that nature.[4] Man, himself, is a part of the coastal environment; he must use that environment without destroying it. And he must rebuild and modify institutions to protect himself from his own, more destructive impulses. It is a challenge which will require the talents of the most skilled and the insight of the wisest men among us.

NOTES

1. E. A. Laurent and J. C. Hite, Resource Management in the Coastal Zone: The Policy Problem, Economics of Marine Resources No. 3, South Carolina Agricultural Experiment Station, Clemson University, Clemson, S. C., April, 1970.

2. Hugh O. Nourse, "The Effect of Air Pollution on House Values," Land Economics, XLIII (May, 1967), p. 187; also T. D. Crocker, Some Economic Aspects of Air Pollution Control with Special Reference to Polk County, Florida, Report to the U.S. Public Health Service, January, 1968.

3. Proceedings of the Twenty-seventh Meeting of the South Carolina Water Resources Commission, Columbia, S.C., September 14, 1970, pp. 4-6.

4. For more discussion on this subject, see James C. Hite, "Comments on Shaffer's Paper on Institutions," in Harold F. Breimyer, ed., Fourteen Variations on a Theme (Columbia: University of Missouri Press, August, 1969).

APPENDIX TABLE 1

Value-Added per $1 of Gross Output and per Employee, Charleston Study Area, 1968

	Value-Added per $1 Gross Output[a]	Value-Added per Employee
1. Agriculture, Forestry, & Fisheries	.4126[c]	2,822
2. Food & Kindred Products	.2655[c]	2,947
3. Construction & Mining	.4130[b]	8,425
4. Textiles & Apparel Mfg.	.3804	1,316
5. Lumber, Pulp, & Paper Prods.	.3430	8,913
6. Furniture & Fixtures Mfg.	.4315	4,248
7. Printers & Publishers	.4700	4,781
8. Chemical Manufacturing	.4680	2,625
9. Petroleum & Coal Mfg.	.2505	392
10. Rubber, Plastic, & Related Mfg.	.4454	1,483
11. Stone, Clay, & Glass Prods. Mfg.	.4902	1,293
12. Machinery & Metal Shops	.4181	3,063
13. Miscellaneous Manufacturing	.4029	2,455
14. Transportation	.6071[b]	4,074
15. Communications	.5141	1,455
16. Utilities	.5606	12,154
17. Eating & Drinking Places	.6175	7,049
18. Hotels & Lodging Places	.6745[b]	2,854
19. Gasoline Service Stations	.4680	21,881
20. Other Wholesale & Retail Trade	.7245	26,263
21. Finance & Insurance	.5602[b]	7,217
22. Real Estate	.7223[b]	21,175
23. Other Business & Professional Services	.5120[b]	2,031
24. Local & State Government	—	—
25. Defense-Related Government	.0000	—
26. Other Federal Government	.0000	—
27. Households	—	—
28. Unallocated	.4001[c]	4,830

[a]Unless specified otherwise, figures are adjusted from value-added coefficients in Robert L. Canion and Warren L. Trock, Input-Output as a Method of Evaluation of the Economic Impact of Water Resource Development, Water Resources Institute, Texas A&M University, May, 1968, pp. 38-39.

[b]Office of Business Economics, Survey of Current Business, U.S. Department of Commerce, Washington, D.C., XXXXIX, 11 (November, 1969).

[c]Charleston Survey

APPENDIX TABLE 2

Value-Added Matrix, Charleston Study Area, 1968

	Agriculture, Forestry, & Fisheries (1)	Food & Kindred Products (2)	Construction & Mining (3)	Textile & Apparel (4)	Lumber & Wood Products (5)	Furniture & Fixtures Mfg. (6)	Printers & Publishers (7)
1. Agriculture, Forestry & Fisheries	.4775	.1119	.0073	.0137	.0286	.0170	.0107
2. Food & Kindred Products	.0050	.3047	.0040	.0045	.0018	.0031	.0043
3. Construction & Mining	.0316	.0259	.8875	.0404	.0263	.0316	.0377
4. Textiles & Apparel Mfg.	.0006	.0013	.0004	.3855	.0002	.0003	.0006
5. Lumber, Pulp, & Paper Prods.	.0024	.0022	.0190	.0028	.3517	.1777	.0027
6. Furniture & Fixtures Mfg.	.0006	.0004	.0005	.0005	.0002	.4318	.0004
7. Printers & Publishers	.0064	.0059	.0051	.0098	.0020	.0035	.5509
8. Chemical Manufacturing	.0016	.0035	.0082	.0022	.0088	.0055	.0103
9. Petroleum & Coal Mfg.	.0001	.0002	.0001	.0001	.0001	.0001	.0001
10. Rubber, Plastic, & Related Mfg.	.0016	.0022	.0059	.0021	.0013	.0014	.0023
11. Stone, Clay, & Glass Prods. Mfg.	.0013	.0011	.0043	.0014	.0006	.0010	.0014
12. Machinery & Metal Shops	.0065	.0031	.0018	.0024	.0012	.0033	.0024
13. Miscellaneous Manufacturing	.0006	.0006	.0024	.0007	.0004	.0009	.0019
14. Transportation	.0100	.0055	.0102	.0078	.0162	.0110	.0059
15. Communications	.0016	.0019	.0016	.0025	.0007	.0013	.0043
16. Utilities	.0103	.0131	.0071	.0098	.0049	.0473	.0092
17. Eating & Drinking Places	.0063	.0056	.0053	.0094	.0027	.0048	.0083
18. Hotels & Lodging Places	.0001	.0001	.0001	.0009	.0001	.0001	.0002
19. Gasoline Service Stations	.0174	.0108	.0070	.0095	.0044	.0074	.0095
20. Other Wholesale & Retail Trade	.5782	.3400	.4259	.3778	.1703	.2799	.3628
21. Finance & Insurance	.0397	.0268	.0273	.0254	.0106	.0241	.0422
22. Real Estate	.0220	.0184	.0224	.0306	.0084	.0154	.0285
23. Other Business & Professional Services	.0709	.0433	.0502	.1402	.0178	.0262	.1049
24. Local & State Government	.0150	.0156	.0119	.0191	.0050	.0086	.0256
25. Defense-Related Government	.0000	.0000	.0000	.0000	.0000	.0000	.0000
26. Other Federal Government	.0000	.0000	.0000	.0000	.0000	.0000	.0000
27. Households	.6991	.6911	.6412	.8687	.3420	.6604	.8707
28. Unallocated	.0093	.0069	.0068	.0177	.0025	.0039	.0140
Local Income Multiplier	2.0157	1.6416	2.1635	1.9855	1.0088	1.7676	2.1118

	Chemical Manufacturing (8)	Petroleum & Coal Mfg. (9)	Rubber, Plastic, & Related Mfg. (10)	Stone, Clay, & Glass Prods. Mfg. (11)	Machinery, Repairs, & Metal Shops (12)	Miscellaneous Manufacturing (13)	Transportation (14)	Communications (15)
1.	.0098	.0050	.0065	.0067	.0048	.0041	.0055	.0032
2.	.0027	.0038	.0035	.0048	.0037	.0035	.0048	.0027
3.	.0282	.0247	.0282	.1085	.1789	.0188	.0561	.0349
4.	.0008	.0004	.0004	.0004	.0004	.0014	.0004	.0002
5.	.0029	.0037	.0024	.0044	.0053	.0044	.0033	.0020
6.	.0030	.0006	.0003	.0005	.0004	.0006	.0005	.0003
7.	.0068	.0042	.0067	.0130	.0042	.0042	.0051	.0048
8.	.5077	.0259	.1130	.0137	.0026	.0046	.0014	.0009
9.	.0000	.2505	.0000	.0001	.0016	.0000	.0001	.0001
10.	.0024	.0011	.4591	.0033	.0020	.0118	.0012	.0007
11.	.0008	.0011	.0011	.4921	.0018	.0008	.0016	.0009
12.	.0014	.0020	.0019	.0027	.4323	.0018	.0026	.0017
13.	.0006	.0004	.0027	.0015	.0033	.4313	.0006	.0003
14.	.0137	.0056	.0066	.0066	.0057	.0034	.6371	.0036
15.	.0038	.0144	.0045	.0020	.0074	.0032	.0032	.5192
16.	.0056	.0068	.0068	.0089	.0257	.0140	.0095	.0095
17.	.0062	.0056	.0006	.0077	.0056	.0041	.0071	.0042
18.	.0001	.0001	.0001	.0002	.0002	.0001	.0002	.0001
19.	.0059	.0082	.0081	.0112	.0085	.0060	.0140	.0073
20.	.2220	.3454	.2904	.4109	.3389	.2145	.4385	.2400
21.	.0179	.0227	.0234	.0271	.0228	.0192	.0267	.0151
22.	.0221	.0181	.0201	.0244	.0187	.0133	.0232	.0263
23.	.1038	.0352	.0570	.0495	.0320	.0275	.0359	.0211
24.	.0085	.0096	.0084	.0114	.0106	.0066	.0114	.0113
25.	.0000	.0000	.0000	.0000	.0000	.0000	.0000	.0000
26.	.0000	.0000	.0000	.0000	.0000	.0000	.0000	.0000
27.	.4767	.7558	.7335	1.0397	.7828	.5533	1.0060	.5817
28.	.0130	.0059	.0078	.0070	.0051	.0039	.0055	.0370
	1.4663	1.5568	1.7931	2.2583	1.9053	1.3564	2.2515	1.5291

(continued)

(APPENDIX TABLE 2, continued)

	Utilities (16)	Eating & Drinking Places (17)	Hotels & Lodging Places (18)	Gasoline Service Stations (19)	Other Wholesale & Retail Trade (20)	Finance & Insurance (21)	Real Estate (22)	Other Bus. & Professional Services (23)
1.	.0037	.0173	.0084	.0039	.0040	.0063	.0099	.0505
2.	.0032	.0427	.0155	.0043	.0054	.0033	.0040	.0058
3.	.0626	.0216	.0311	.0183	.0108	.0837	.7175	.0894
4.	.0003	.0004	.0004	.0010	.0004	.0009	.0007	.0025
5.	.0025	.0015	.0023	.0015	.0013	.0035	.0158	.0032
6.	.0005	.0004	.0006	.0006	.0009	.0003	.0005	.0005
7.	.0032	.0030	.0042	.0031	.0029	.0133	.0073	.0316
8.	.0014	.0012	.0021	.0012	.0012	.0020	.0078	.0066
9.	.0001	.0001	.0002	.0010	.0000	.0000	.0001	.0001
10.	.0010	.0010	.0012	.0011	.0013	.0024	.0056	.0062
11.	.0009	.0007	.0011	.0006	.0003	.0012	.0036	.0011
12.	.0216	.0023	.0023	.0013	.0007	.0019	.0018	.0023
13.	.0007	.0003	.0004	.0003	.0002	.0009	.0021	.0006
14.	.0053	.0055	.0073	.0088	.0115	.0049	.0093	.0090
15.	.0015	.0012	.0022	.0012	.0007	.0070	.0026	.0024
16.	.5691	.0338	.0223	.0057	.0061	.0064	.0076	.0187
17.	.0038	.6207	.0048	.0030	.0019	.0056	.0062	.0211
18.	.0001	.0064	.6757	.0001	.0001	.0001	.0001	.0003
19.	.0056	.0051	.0072	.4728	.0024	.0073	.0069	.0069
20.	.3454	.3801	.5064	.5942	.8451	.3041	.4122	.4726
21.	.0157	.0146	.0238	.0164	.0150	.7217	.0463	.0347
22.	.0123	.0108	.0157	.0103	.0074	.0775	.7614	.0725
23.	.0249	.0227	.0281	.0240	.0209	.0542	.0850	.5987
24.	.0238	.0394	.0278	.0202	.0188	.0088	.0150	.0213
25.	.0000	.0000	.0000	.0000	.0000	.0000	.0000	.0000
26.	.0000	.0000	.0000	.0000	.0000	.0000	.0000	.0000
27.	.5085	.4224	.6536	.3758	.2094	.6659	.6199	.5381
28.	.0038	.0036	.0044	.0035	.0030	.0077	.0110	.0711
	1.5977	1.6588	2.0491	1.5707	1.1717	1.9909	2.7447	2.0678

	Local & State Government (24)	Defense- Related Government (25)	Other Federal Government (26)	Households (27)	Unallocated (28)
1.	.0070	.0057	.0059	.0061	.0020
2.	.0054	.0049	.0045	.0053	.0008
3.	.0825	.0725	.1087	.0353	.1340
4.	.0005	.0004	.0004	.0004	.0002
5.	.0042	.0038	.0044	.0033	.0033
6.	.0007	.0005	.0005	.0005	.0005
7.	.0066	.0052	.0092	.0056	.0014
8.	.0025	.0017	.0025	.0013	.0015
9.	.0008	.0001	.0002	.0001	.0002
10.	.0015	.0014	.0016	.0012	.0011
11.	.0020	.0018	.0018	.0018	.0007
12.	.0035	.0028	.0041	.0031	.0003
13.	.0007	.0006	.0016	.0006	.0004
14.	.0083	.0064	.0064	.0066	.0021
15.	.0026	.0018	.0029	.0020	.0005
16.	.0121	.0102	.0147	.0096	.0017
17.	.0081	.0075	.0072	.0084	.0023
18.	.0004	.0002	.0016	.0002	.0001
19.	.0129	.0116	.0107	.0130	.0014
20.	.4419	.4287	.3920	.4502	.0730
21.	.0297	.0260	.0592	.0292	.0089
22.	.0350	.0234	.0261	.0257	.1400
23.	.0505	.0369	.0414	.0394	.0169
24.	1.0292	.0109	.0114	.0114	.0036
25.	.0000	.0000	.0000	.0000	.0000
26.	.0000	.0000	.0000	.0000	.0000
27.	1.0803	1.0764	.9849	1.2054	.1201
28.	.0201	.0056	.0081	.0060	.4302
	2.8289	1.7470	1.7113	1.8717	.9472

Source: Calculated by multiplying data in Appendix Table 1 by the appropriate row in Table 5.

JAMES C. HITE is Associate Professor in the Department of Agricultural Economics and Rural Sociology at Clemson University, Clemson, South Carolina. He holds an M. A. in history from Emory University and a Ph. D. in agricultural economics from Clemson University. In 1969 and 1970 he was a post doctoral scholar with the Regional Science Group at Harvard University. Professor Hite is co-editor of Coastal Zone Resource Management, published in 1971, and he has contributed numerous articles to professional journals.

EUGENE A. LAURENT is Assistant Professor in the Environmental Resources Center at Georgia Institute of Technology, Atlanta. He holds an M. S. from the University of Nebraska and a Ph. D. from Clemson University in agricultural economics. In 1969 he was a member of the South Carolina Task Force on Tidelands Planning and has published numerous articles in scholarly journals.